Federal Health Centers

Elayne J. Heisler
Analyst in Health Services

March 21, 2012

Congressional Research Service

7-5700
www.crs.gov
R42433

CRS Report for Congress ————————————
Prepared for Members and Committees of Congress

Summary

The federal health center program, authorized in Section 330 of the Public Health Service Act, awards grants to support health centers: outpatient primary care facilities that provide care to primarily low-income individuals. The program—administered by the Health Resources and Services Administration (HRSA) within the Department of Health and Human Services (HHS)—supports four types of health centers: (1) community health centers; (2) health centers for the homeless; (3) health centers for residents of public housing; and (4) migrant health centers. According to HRSA data, there are over 8,633 unique health center sites (i.e., unique health center facility locations). Facilities must meet a number of requirements to receive a Section 330 grant, but receiving these grants enables health centers to receive services or in-kind benefits from a number of federal programs.

Appropriations for the health center program have increased over the past decade, resulting in more centers and more patients served. From FY2000 through FY2012 the health center program's appropriation increased by 48%. Over this same time period, the number of health center sites increased by 59%. The program also received supplemental appropriations through the American Recovery and Reinvestment Act (P.L. 111-5) in FY2009. The program's expansion may continue under the Patient Protection and Affordable Care Act of 2010 (P.L. 111-148, ACA), which permanently authorized the health center program and created the Community Health Center Fund (CHCF) that included a total of $9.5 billion for health center operations to be appropriated in FY2011 through FY2015. However, it is not clear whether these funds will be used to expand the health center program because in FY2011, FY2012, and the FY2013 President's Budget request, these funds were or would be used to augment discretionary appropriation reductions to the health center program.

Health centers are required to provide health care to all individuals regardless of their ability to pay and are required to be located in geographic areas that have few health care providers. These requirements make health centers part of the health safety net—providers that serve the uninsured, the underserved, or those enrolled in Medicaid. Data compiled by HRSA demonstrate that health centers serve the intended safety net population as the majority of patients are uninsured or enrolled in Medicaid. Some research also suggests that health centers are a cost effective way of meeting this population's health needs because researchers have found that patients seen at health centers have lower health care costs than those served in other settings. In general, research has found that health centers, among other outcomes, improve health, reduce costs, and provide access to health care for populations that may otherwise not obtain health care.

This report provides an overview of the federal health center program including its statutory authority, program requirements, and appropriation levels. The report then describes health centers in general, where they are located, their patient population, and some outcomes associated with health center use. It also describes some federal programs available to assist health center operations including the federally qualified health center (FQHC) designation for Medicare and Medicaid payments. The report then concludes with a brief discussion of issues for Congress such as the potential effects of the ACA on health centers, the health center workforce, and financial considerations for health centers in the context of changing federal and state budgets. Finally, the report has two appendixes that describe (1) FQHC payments for Medicare and Medicaid beneficiaries served at health centers; and (2) programs that are similar to health centers but not authorized in Section 330 of the PHSA.

Contents

Figures

Tables

Appendixes

Contacts

Introduction

The federal health center program awards grants to support health centers: outpatient primary care facilities that provide care to primarily low-income individuals. The program is administered by the Health Resources and Services Administration (HRSA)—within its Bureau of Primary Care—within the Department of Health and Human Services (HHS). The federal health center program is authorized in Section 330 of the Public Health Service Act (PHSA) and supports four types of health centers: (1) community health centers; (2) health centers for the homeless; (3) health centers for residents of public housing; and (4) migrant health centers.

According to HRSA data there are over 8,633 unique health center sites (i.e., individual health center facility locations);[1] the majority are community health centers (CHCs). CHCs serve the general low income or otherwise disadvantaged population whereas the remaining three types of health centers provide care to more targeted low income or otherwise disadvantaged populations (e.g., migrant health workers). Regardless of type, health centers are required, by statute, to provide health care to all individuals regardless of their ability to pay and are required to be located in geographic areas that have few health care providers.[2] These requirements make health centers part of the health safety net—providers that serve the uninsured, the underserved, or those enrolled in Medicaid.[3] Data compiled by HRSA demonstrate that health centers serve the intended safety net population as the majority of patients are uninsured or enrolled in Medicaid.[4] Some research also suggests that health centers are a cost effective way of meeting this population's health needs because researchers have found that patients seen at health centers have lower health care costs than those served in other settings.[5] Others have found that areas with health centers have lower emergency room use and fewer hospital stays.[6] Researchers have also found that care provided in emergency departments and physicians' offices is generally more costly than care provided at health centers.[7] In general, research has found that health centers' presence is associated with several outcomes, most notably improved health, reduced costs, and increased access to health care for populations that may otherwise not obtain health care.[8]

---

[1] The Health Resources and Services Administration regularly updates health center data. This report uses the number of sites as of 1/17/2012, see http://datawarehouse.hrsa.gov/sitesdetail.aspx; hereinafter *HRSA Data Warehouse*.

[2] 42 U.S.C. §254b.

[3] Lewin, Marion Ein and Altman, Stuart, *America's Health Care Safety Net: Intact but Endangered*, Institute of Medicine, Washington, DC, 2000, p. 21, http://www.nap.edu/catalog.php?record_id=9612; for more information on the Medicaid program, see CRS Report RL33202, *Medicaid: A Primer*, by Elicia J. Herz.

[4] Health Resources and Services Administration, Bureau of Primary Care, *Uniform Data System*, 2010 National Summary Report, Rockville, MD, July 27, 2011, http://bphc.hrsa.gov/uds/doc/2010/National_Universal.pdf. Hereinafter, *2010 UDS Report*.

[5] Patrick Richard et al., "Cost Savings Associated with the Use of Community Health Centers," *Journal of Ambulatory Care Management*, vol. 35, no. 1 (2012), pp. 50-59.

[6] George Rust, et al. "Presence of a Community Health Center and Uninsured Emergency Department Visits Rates in Rural Counties," *The Journal of Rural Health*, vol.25, no. 1 (Winter 2009), pp, 8-16; Betty Smith-Campbell, "Emergency Department and Community Health Center Visits and Costs in an Uninsured Population," *Journal of Nursing Scholarship,* (First Quarter 2005), vol.37, no. 1; and Jack Hadley and Peter Cunningham, "Availability of Safety Net Providers and Access to Care for Uninsured Persons," *Health Services Research*, vol. 39, no.5 (October 2004), pp. 1527-1546.

[7] Ibid.

[8] This research is summarized in the report section below: "What Outcomes Are Associated with Health Center Use?"

Section 330 grants—funded by the health center program's appropriation—are estimated to only cover one-fifth of an individual health center's operating costs; however, individual health centers are eligible for grants or payments from a number of federal programs to supplement their facilities' budgets.[9] These federal programs provide (1) incentives to recruit and retain providers; (2) access to higher reimbursement rates from the Medicare, Medicaid, and State Children's Health Insurance (CHIP) programs;[10] (3) access to additional funding through federal programs that target populations generally served by health centers; and (4) in-kind support such as access to discounted or free services that a health center may otherwise have to purchase at a higher rate (e.g., prescription drug discounts or medical malpractice insurance). These additional programs are important for individual health centers because more than one-third of all health center program grantees rely on a federal program to recruit providers,[11] and Medicaid is the largest source of health center reimbursements.[12] Other federal grants (i.e., non-330 grants) are also an important source of financial support for health centers; in FY2011 health centers funded under the health center program received approximately $230 million—which is roughly equivalent to 9% of the program's annual appropriation[13]—in other federal grants.[14]

Appropriations to support the health center program have increased over the past decade. These increases began in 2000 and continued with supplemental funding appropriated under the American Recovery and Reinvestment Act (ARRA, P.L. 111-5) and the Patient Protection and Affordable Care Act of 2010 (ACA, P.L. 111-148).[15] Congress has appropriated additional funds for the program, which have generally been used to award grants to create new centers.[16] In addition, ARRA and the ACA appropriated funds have supported health center construction and renovation. Some ARRA funds were also used to increase services provided at existing centers.[17] The ACA also appropriated funding for health centers to train medical residents.[18] Although the

---

[9] U.S. Department of Health and Human Services, Health Resources and Services Administration, Bureau of Primary Health Care, *Efforts to Expand and Accelerate Health Center Program Quality Improvement*, Report to Congress, Rockville, MD; hereinafter, *Health Center Quality Improvement Report*.

[10] These payments are discussed in more detail in **Appendix B**; payments are considered to be "higher" than the payment rates that physician practices receive because they are cost-based and reflect a broader range of services, than do payments to physician practices. See, for example, Department of Health Policy, School of Public Health and Health Services, The George Washington University, *Quality Incentives for Federally Qualified Health Centers, Rural Health Clinics and Free Clinics: A Report to Congress*, Washington, DC, January 23, 2012.

[11] Roger A. Rosenblatt et al., "Shortages of Medical Personnel at Community Health Centers: Implications for Planned Expansion," *Journal of the American Medical Association*, vol. 295, no. 9 (March 2006), pp. 1042-1049.

[12] 2010 UDS Report.

[13] See **Table 3** and **Table 4**.

[14] See **Table 4**.

[15] The ACA was subsequently amended by the Health Care and Education Reconciliation Act (HCERA, P.L. 111-152). These two laws are collectively referred to as the ACA in this report. Previous CRS reports on the Patient Protection and Affordable Care Act used the acronym PPACA to refer to the statute. This report will use "ACA," in conformance with the more widely-used acronym for the law.

[16] See discussion in CRS Report R40181, *Selected Health Funding in the American Recovery and Reinvestment Act of 2009*, coordinated by C. Stephen Redhead, and CRS Report R41278, *Public Health, Workforce, Quality, and Related Provisions in PPACA: Summary and Timeline*, coordinated by C. Stephen Redhead and Erin D. Williams. The ACA also authorized new grant programs to provide funding for facilities that are similar to health centers—nurse managed health clinics and school-based health centers. These facilities will provide care to populations similar to those served by health centers, but are not authorized in PHSA Section 330. These facilities and other facilities that are similar to health centers are summarized in **Appendix A**.

[17] CRS Report R40181, *Selected Health Funding in the American Recovery and Reinvestment Act of 2009*, coordinated by C. Stephen Redhead.

[18] CRS Report R41301, *Appropriations and Fund Transfers in the Patient Protection and Affordable Care Act* (continued...)

---

program's appropriations increased by 48% since FY2000, the additional appropriated funds have generally been used to expand the number of centers—which increased by 59%[19]—while funding awarded to individual centers increased less rapidly over the time period.[20]

The ACA aims to expand insurance coverage to the uninsured, which may have a number of effects on health centers. Specifically, the law aims to reduce the number of uninsured by expanding the Medicaid program and by providing subsidies for certain low income individuals to purchase health insurance coverage.[21] These changes may have a number of effects on individual health centers. First, they may mean that more individuals may seek care at health centers. This may occur because health centers are a source of care for the uninsured and those enrolled in Medicaid because they are required to accept all patients regardless of ability to pay.[22] Health centers may continue to serve those who obtain insurance under the ACA because some may choose to remain with their providers and because health centers are located in areas with few health care providers. It is also possible that health center reimbursements may increase as fewer people remain uninsured. The ACA also includes a new direct appropriation that is a significant investment in health centers, which may help these health centers provide care to an expanded population; however, given recent fiscal concerns, these funds have not been used to significantly expand the health center appropriation.[23]

This report provides an overview of the federal health center program including its statutory authority, program requirements, and appropriation levels. The report then describes health centers in general, where they are located, their patient population, and some outcomes associated with health center use. It also describes the federal programs available to assist health center operations including the federally qualified health center (FQHC) designation for Medicare and Medicaid payments. The report then concludes with a brief discussion of issues for Congress such as the potential effects of the ACA on health centers (both the program and individual health centers), the health center workforce, and financial considerations for health centers in the context of changing federal and state budgets. Finally, the report has two appendices that describe (1) FQHC payments for Medicare and Medicaid beneficiaries served at health centers; and (2) programs that are similar to health centers but not authorized in Section 330 of the PHSA.

(...continued)

(PPACA), by C. Stephen Redhead, and CRS Report R41278, *Public Health, Workforce, Quality, and Related Provisions in PPACA: Summary and Timeline*, coordinated by C. Stephen Redhead and Erin D. Williams.

[19] See **Table 3**.

[20] CRS analysis of HRSA Budget documents.

[21] CRS Report R41664, *ACA: A Brief Overview of the Law, Implementation, and Legal Challenges*, coordinated by C. Stephen Redhead, and CRS Report R41210, *Medicaid and the State Children's Health Insurance Program (CHIP) Provisions in ACA: Summary and Timeline*, by Evelyne P. Baumrucker et al.

[22] They are also a major source of care for Medicaid patients because some providers will not accept Medicaid because of low reimbursements rates or administrative requirements of the program, see Jack Hadley and Peter Cunningham, "Availability of Safety Net Providers and Access to Care of Uninsured Persons," *Health Services Research*, vol. 39, no. 5 (October 2004), pp. 1527-1546 and Peter J. Cunningham and Ann S. O'Malley, "Do Reimbursement Delays Discourage Medicaid Participation by Physicians?" *Health Affairs*, vol. 28, no. 1 (November 18, 2008), p. w17–w28.

[23] See discussion of CHCF in Appendix A of CRS Report R41737, *Public Health Service (PHS) Agencies: Overview and Funding, FY2010-FY2012*, coordinated by C. Stephen Redhead and Pamela W. Smith.

What Is the Federal Health Center Program?

The federal health center program awards grants to support outpatient primary care facilities that provide care to primarily low income individuals. The program is authorized in Section 330 of the PHSA, which also includes definitions of the four types of health centers[24] and program requirements. This section describes the statutory authority for the federal health center program (also called the health center program); program requirements; types of grants awarded in support of the health center program; the health center program's appropriation; and other funding/revenue that health centers receive.

Statutory Authority and General Requirements[25]

Section 330 of the PHSA authorizes grants for health centers and includes the requirements for entities to receive a health center grant. Section 330 requires health centers to provide services to the entire population of their service area regardless of ability to pay. Health centers are also required to document the health needs of the residents in their service area and to update their service area if needed. Health center grantees must (1) be located in specific geographic areas; (2) have an established fee schedule that meets certain requirements; (3) collect reimbursements for individuals enrolled in public or private insurance programs; (4) have appropriate governance; (5) offer specific health services; (6) meet certain reporting and quality assurance requirements; and (7) license providers and seek accreditation. This section describes each of these requirements.

Location Requirements

PHSA Section 330 requires that a health center be located in an area that is designated as medically underserved or as serving a population designated as "Medically Underserved" (see **text box**).[26]

Medically Underserved Areas/Populations

Medically Underserved Areas (MUA): Areas of varying size—whole counties, groups of contiguous counties, civil divisions, or a group of urban census tracts—where residents have a shortage of health care services.

Medically Underserved Populations (MUPs): Groups that face economic, cultural, or linguistic barriers to accessing health care.

Source: HRSA, Bureau of Primary Care, Shortage Designations, at http://bhpr.hrsa.gov/shortage/index.htm.

---

[24] These definitions and more information about the number and types of services that the four types of health centers provide are discussed in the report section "What Types of Health Centers Exist?"

[25] HRSA details the program's requirements on its website at http://bphc.hrsa.gov/about/requirements/index.html. The subsections that follow refer to this website in addition to the citations noted below.

[26] Section 5602 of the Patient Protection and Affordable Care Act (ACA, P.L. 111-148) required the Secretary of HHS to revise the criteria and methodology used to designate health professional shortage areas (HPSAs) and MUPs. The ACA also required that HHS appoint a committee to undertake this revision and publish a final rule with the new criteria. The Committee released a report on October 1, 2011, see http://www.hrsa.gov/advisorycommittees/shortage/nrmcfinalreport.pdf.

Fee Schedule Requirements

Health centers must establish their own fee schedules that take into account local rates for health services and the costs that the health center incurs providing services. The health center is then required to establish a separate discounted fee schedule, which is then further discounted or waived based on a patient's ability to pay. Ability to pay is determined by the patient's income relative to the federal poverty level. The statute requires that individuals whose income is above 200% of the federal poverty level pay full charges, while individuals whose incomes are at, or below, 100% of the federal poverty level pay only nominal fees.[27]

Medicaid Coordination and Reimbursement Requirements

Health centers are required to coordinate with state Medicaid and CHIP plans to provide services to beneficiaries enrolled in these programs. They are also required to seek reimbursement from third party payers such as private insurance plans, Medicare, Medicaid, and CHIP. Health centers are further required to have systems to obtain reimbursements including those used for billing, credit, and collections. These collections provide nearly two-thirds of the health center program's revenue (see **Table 4**).

Although health centers collect reimbursements, the Government Accountability Office (GAO) found that Medicare payments did not cover the full cost of health center services in nearly two-thirds of the visits they examined.[28] Similarly, the National Association of Community Health Centers (NACHC)—the advocacy group for health centers—reports that the amount received in reimbursements is not sufficient to cover the cost of the health services provided.[29] They found that Medicaid reimbursements covered 85% of the cost of providing services, while Medicare and private insurance reimbursements cover less than two-thirds.[30] The NACHC also found that the PHSA Section 330 grant amount received per patient—$270—was less than the average medical cost per patient of $414.[31]

Governance Requirements

Health centers are required to have a governing board that is primarily made up of health center patients. The governing board provides input on center operational issues including the center's budget, operating hours, management, and oversight. It is required to meet monthly, and must approve the center's director and must approve grant applications submitted by the center.[32]

---

[27] 42 C.F. R. 51c.303(f) and Section 330(k)(3)(G)(i) of the Public Health Service Act (PHSA).

[28] U.S. Government Accountability Office, *Medicare Payments to Federally Qualified Health Centers*, GAO-10-576R, July 30, 2010. **Appendix B** describes ACA changes to Medicare FQHC payments that may more closely align Medicare payments to the costs of providing services.

[29] See National Association of Community Health Centers, *A Sketch of Community Health Centers*, Chartbook, Washington, DC, 2009, http://www.nachc.com/client/documents/Chartbook%20FINAL%202009.pdf; hereinafter, *2009 Health Center Chartbook*.

[30] Ibid.

[31] Ibid; this amount does not include lab, x-ray, or nurse visits.

[32] 42 U.S.C. §254b; some governance requirements may be waived for migrant health centers, health centers for the homeless, and health centers for residents of public housing.

Health Service Requirements

Health centers are required to provide primary care services (as defined in Section 330 of the PHSA and discussed below) and may also provide behavioral health services, case management, and specialty care services. This section discusses the required services, certain optional services, and then presents some data on services provided at health centers in 2010. (See **Table 1**.)

Health centers are required to provide primary health services and preventive and emergency health services.[33] Primary health services are those provided by physicians[34] or physician extenders (physicians' assistants, nurse clinicians, and nurse practitioners) to diagnose, treat, or refer patients. Primary health services include relevant diagnostic laboratory and radiology services. Preventive health services include well-child care, prenatal and postpartum care, immunization, family planning, health education, and preventive dental care. Emergency health services refer to the requirement that health centers have defined arrangements with outside providers for emergent cases that the center is not equipped to treat and for after-hours care. Health center providers must also have admitting privileges at one or more hospitals located near the health center. This requirement is to ensure care continuity for hospitalized health center patients. In instances where a health center physician does not have admitting privileges at a nearby hospital, the health center is required to establish other arrangements to ensure care continuity. In addition to these three types of services (primary, preventive, and emergency), health centers must provide diabetes self-management training for patients with diabetes or renal disease.[35]

Health centers are also required to provide enabling services such as transportation for individuals residing in each center's service area who have difficulty accessing the center, translation services, and health education. Health centers may also provide supplemental services such as additional dental care, mental health services, or substance abuse treatment.[36] **Table 1** describes some specific services tracked in the Uniform Data System (UDS) 2010 data, the most recent year of final data available.

---

[33] 42 CFR 51c.102(h).

[34] The regulation further specifies that these services should be provided by primary care physicians who are defined as physicians in family practice, internal medicine, pediatrics, or obstetrics and gynecology.

[35] This requirement was added by P.L. 109-171, effective January 1, 2006.

[36] For specific types of health centers (see "What Types of Health Centers Exist?") some of supplemental services may be required.

Table 1. Examples of Services Provided and the Number of Patients Served by Health Centers (2010)

Service Provided	Number of Patients Served
Medical Services	16,777,152
Enabling Services	1,793,746
Dental Services	3,750,481
Substance Abuse Services	98,760
Mental Health Services	852,984

Source: HRSA, Uniform Data System (UDS) Report, UDS, National Rollup Report, 2010 at http://bphc.hrsa.gov/uds/doc/2010/National_Universal.pdf and National Total Summary Data at http://bphc.hrsa.gov/uds/view.aspx?year=2010; hereinafter, 2010 UDS Report.

Reporting and Quality Assurance Requirements

Health centers are required to report to HRSA certain information and to have quality improvement and assurance plans in place. First, health centers are required to report patient demographics, services provided, staffing information, utilization rates, costs, and revenue to HRSA's UDS. Second, within the UDS, health centers must report on certain clinical outcomes to assess quality.[37] These outcomes are similar to those examined in other health care settings. They include, for example, the percentage of children receiving recommended immunizations by the age of two; percentage of women who were screened for cervical cancer; and the percentage of patients whose body mass index was assessed and were referred to appropriate services if found to be obese.[38] Finally, health centers are required to have quality improvement systems in place that include clinical services, management, and patient confidentiality assurances. To meet this requirement, health centers must have a clinical director who reports on quality improvement and assurance activities and conducts periodic assessments of the health center's services to evaluate the quality and appropriateness of services provided.

Licensing and Accreditation Requirements

Health center providers must be properly licensed in the state in which they practice. They must also have admitting privileges at hospitals that health center patients would likely be referred to (see "Health Service Requirements"). Furthermore, they must maintain proper credentials during their health center employment.

Health centers are not required to be accredited by a national accreditation agency, but HRSA encourages health centers to seek accreditation. Specifically, the agency encourages health centers to seek accreditation from either the Accreditation Association for Ambulatory Health

---

[37] Such as performance measures and clinical outcomes commonly used by the Medicare and Medicaid programs, and health insurance and managed care organizations. For more information, see http://bphc.hrsa.gov/policiesregulations/performancemeasures/index.html.

[38] Ibid. HRSA also submitted a report to Congress about ongoing health center quality improvement efforts; see U.S. Department of Health and Human Services, Health Resources and Services Administration, Bureau of Primary Care, *Report to Congress: Efforts to Expand and Accelerate Health Center Program Quality Improvement*, Rockville, MD, April 26, 2011, http://bphc.hrsa.gov/ftca/riskmanagement/healthcenterqualityimprovement.pdf; herein after, *Health Center Quality Improvement Report*.

Care (AAHC) or The Joint Commission (TJC). HRSA will pay some of the costs of seeking and maintaining accreditation from one of these two accrediting entities.[39]

Grants that Support Federal Health Centers

HRSA awards five types of Section 330 authorized grants to support health centers: (1) grants for new health centers; (2) grants to expand services at existing health centers; (3) grants for construction and renovation; (4) planning grants; and (5) grants to reduce infant mortality. This section describes these types of grants, the entities that are eligible to receive grants, and the factors taken into consideration when awarding grants.

Types of Grants Available to Support Health Centers

The first type of grants awarded is called New Access Point (NAP) grants and permits existing grantees to establish new sites or new grantees to establish new health centers. The second type of grants is called Increased Demand for Services (IDS) or Expanded Service (ES) grants. These grants are for health centers to expand the number of patients they serve or to provide additional types of services. The third type of grants is awarded through the Capital Improvement Program (CIP) and provides funding for the construction and renovation of health centers. These grants were supported with ARRA appropriated funds and with ACA appropriated funds in FY2011.[40] The fourth type of grants is for entities that are not health centers, to plan and develop health centers. Funds awarded may be used for assessing the health needs of the proposed service population and developing linkages with the community and with health providers in the proposed service area. ACA funds supported these grants in FY2011.[41] The fifth grant program supports activities that aim to reduce infant mortality. These grants have not been awarded in recent years; instead, HRSA supports other infant mortality reduction programs.[42]

Grant Eligibility and Awarding Criteria

Public and non-profit entities are eligible to apply for Section 330 grants to operate health centers. The majority of health center grantees operate facilities at more than one site and may operate more than one type of health center.[43] Grants are awarded competitively based on an assessment of the need for services in a given area and the merit of the application submitted. Grants may also be awarded based on certain funding priorities such as creating a rural-urban balance in health center locations and ensuring that health centers are located in sparsely populated areas.[44]

---

[39] For more information, see http://bphc.hrsa.gov/policiesregulations/accreditation.html/.

[40] See discussion in CRS Report R40181, *Selected Health Funding in the American Recovery and Reinvestment Act of 2009*, coordinated by C. Stephen Redhead, and CRS Report R41278, *Public Health, Workforce, Quality, and Related Provisions in PPACA: Summary and Timeline*, coordinated by C. Stephen Redhead and Erin D. Williams.

[41] In FY2011, ACA-appropriated funds were also used to support planning grants for entities seeking to become health centers; see U.S. Department of Health and Human Services, "HHS Awards Affordable Care Act Funds for Organizations to Become Community Health Centers," press release, September 15, 2011, http://www.hhs.gov/news/press/2011pres/09/20110915d.html.

[42] For more information about these programs, see CRS Report R41378, *The U.S. Infant Mortality Rate: International Comparisons, Underlying Factors, and Federal Programs*, by Elayne J. Heisler.

[43] Health Center Quality Improvement Report.

[44] Department of Health and Human Services, Health Resources and Services Administration, *Justification of Estimations for Appropriations Committees*, FY2012, Rockville, MD; hereinafter, *HRSA FY2012 Budget Justification* (continued...)

Grant recipients are not required to provide matching funds, but are required to use grant funds to supplement and not supplant funding that had been available prior to the grant. Grant amounts awarded are determined based on the cost of proposed grant activity (see **Table 2**). An entity may receive funding for multi-year projects, but amounts awarded in subsequent years are contingent on (1) congressional appropriations and (2) the entity's compliance with applicable statutory, regulatory, and reporting requirements. At the end of the application period, health centers are required to compete for continued funding.[45]

Table 2. Health Center Grants Awarded in FY2011

Grants	FY2011
Total	1,134
Average Size	$2 million
Range of Awarded Amounts	$250 thousand-$13 million

Source: HRSA FY2013 Budget Justification.

What Is the Health Center Program's Appropriation?

The health center program's appropriation has increased over the past decade, resulting in more centers and more patients served. From FY2000 through FY2012 (the last year of final appropriation information available) the health center appropriation increased by 48%. Over this same time period, the number of health center sites increased by 59%. Beginning in 2002, the George W. Bush Administration began a multi-year effort to expand the health center program by providing funding for new or expanded health centers for 1,200 communities.[46] The program's expansion continued during the Obama Administration. In FY2009, under the Obama Administration, the health center program received $2 billion under ARRA. Specifically, ARRA provided $500 million for new sites and expanded services at existing sites. It also provided $1.5 billion for construction, renovation, equipment, and health information technology. The program's expansion may continue under the ACA, which permanently authorized the health center program; appropriated a total of $1.5 billion for health center construction and repair; and created the Community Health Center Fund (CHCF) that included a total of $9.5 billion for health center operations to be appropriated in FY2011 through FY2015. However, it is not clear whether these funds will be used to expand the health center program because in FY2011, FY2012, and the FY2013 President's Budget request, these funds were or would be used to augment reductions to discretionary appropriations to the health center program.[47]

(...continued)

and Department of Health and Human Services, Health Resources and Services Administration, *Justification of Estimations for Appropriations Committees, FY2013, Rockville, MD;* hereinafter, *HRSA FY2013 Budget Justification.*

[45] Ibid.

[46] Department of Health and Human Services, *Budget in Brief,* FY2007, pp. 5-6 and 21.

[47] Under the ACA, the CHCF was required to be used to increase the health center appropriation level above the FY2008 appropriations level; however, P.L. 112-10, which provided full-year funding in FY2011, removed this requirement and some of the CHCF was used to augment discretionary funding for the health center program. The same thing occurred in FY2012. The 112th Congress has also considered rescinding the CHCF in H.R. 3070, which would have provided full year appropriations for FY2012.

Table 3 presents the health center program's appropriation from FY2002 through the FY2013 Request. The table also includes amounts appropriated under ARRA and the ACA and the number of grantees in each fiscal year.

Table 3. Health Center Appropriations and Sites, FY2002-FY2013 (President's Budget Request)

(Dollars in Millions)

	2002	2003	2004	2005	2006	2007	2008	2009	2009 ARRA[a] Funds	2010	2011	2011 ACA CHCF[b] Transfer	2012	2012 ACA CHCF Transfer[b]	2013 President's Budget Request	2013 ACA CHCF Transfer[b]
Health center appropriations	$1,343	$1,505	$1,617	$1,735	$1,785	$1,988	$2,065	$2,190	$2,000	$2,185	$2,581[d]	$1,000	$2,767[c]	$1,200	$3,062[c]	$1,500
Change in appropriations from previous year	+$174	+$162	+$112	+$118	+$50	+$203	+$77	+$2,126[d]	N/A	-$2,005	+$396[c]	N/A	+$186[c]	+$200[c]	+295[c]	+300[c]
Approximate number of sites	3,488	3,578	3,651	3,745	3,831	—[e]	6,208	7,892	7,892	8,156	8,501[f]	N/A	8,746[f]	N/A	8,746[f]	N/A

Source: Compiled by CRS from Health Resources and Services Administration budget documents and H.Rept. 112-331 on P.L. 112-74.

Note: Appropriated amounts include federal tort claims funds.

a. American Recovery and Reinvestment Act (ARRA, P.L. 111-5).

b. Community Health Center Fund (CHCF) created in Section 10503 of the Patient Protection and Affordable Care Act of 2010 (ACA, P.L. 111-148).

c. Includes CHCF transfer.

d. Includes ARRA funding.

e. Number not included in HRSA budget documents.

f. Number estimated in the FY2013 HRSA Budget Justification.

What Are the Other Sources of Funding for the Health Center Program?

In addition to amounts received from grants authorized under the program's annual appropriation (i.e., Section 330 grants), health centers receive funding from reimbursements and funding from other sources (e.g., state and local grants). The relative contribution of each of these sources to an individual health center's budget varies by center. However, the HRSA compiles this information for the health center program. **Table 4** presents data for FY2011, the most recent year of final data available. The table shows that Medicaid is the largest source of health center revenue (38%) and that Section 330 grants provide approximately 20% of the program's revenue. The table also shows that amounts received from grants and contracts from state, local, and private foundations provided nearly 17.6% of the program's total revenue in FY2011. (See **Table 4**.)

Table 4. Health Center Revenue Sources (FY2011)

(Dollars in Millions)

Funding Sources	Dollars	Percent of Program Revenue
Section 330 Authorized Grants		
Section 330 Grants	2,480.0	19.5
Total (Section 330 authorized grants)	**2,480.9**	**19.5**
Reimbursements		
Medicaid	4,830.0	38.0
CHIP	760.0	6.0
Medicare	300.0	2.4
Other third party payers (e.g., private insurance)	1,100.0	8.7
Patient Fees[a]	765.0	6.0
Total (Reimbursements)	**7,755.0**	**61.0**
Other Federal Grants		
Other Federal Grants	230.0	1.8
Total (Other Federal Grants)	**230.0**	**1.8**
State, Local, and Private Grants and Contracts		
State, Local, Other	2,240.0	17.6
Total (State, Local, and Private Grants and Contracts)	**2,240.0**	**17.6**
Total (all sources)	**12,705.9**	**N/A**

Source: HRSA FY2013 Budget Justification.

Note: Percentages may not sum to 100% due to rounding.

a. This refers to amounts collected from self-pay patients.

What Are Health Centers?

This section describes health center facilities funded under the health center program appropriation. It includes a discussion of the four types of health centers funded and compares the services offered and population served by each center type. The section also describes (1) the populations served by the four types of health centers; (2) where health centers are located; and (3) outcomes associated with health center use.[48]

What Types of Health Centers Exist?

There are four types of health centers: (1) community health centers; (2) health centers for the homeless; (3) health centers for residents of public housing; and (4) migrant health centers. The majority of health centers are community health centers (CHCs), which serve a generally underserved population. The other three types of health centers serve more targeted populations, including the homeless, residents of public housing, and migrant workers (Health Centers for the Homeless, Health Centers for Residents of Public Housing, and Migrant Health Centers, respectively). This section describes each type of health center, the population targeted by these centers, and the specific services that each type of center must provide.[49]

Community Health Centers

The majority of health centers are CHCs because these facilities serve the general population with limited access to health care. CHCs are required to serve all residents who reside in the area that the CHC serves (this is also known as the catchment area). CHCs are required to provide "primary health services" (see "Health Service Requirements"). The CHC-required services are the baseline services that all types of health centers are required to provide. The other three types of health centers may be required to provide certain supplemental services that aim to meet the specific needs of the population they serve.

Health Centers for the Homeless

Health Centers for the Homeless (HCHs) provide services to homeless individuals; it is the only federal health program that targets this generally uninsured population.[50] Section 330 defines homeless individuals as those who lack permanent housing or live in temporary facilities or transitional housing.[51] In addition to the services required of all health centers, HCHs are required to provide substance abuse services and supportive services that aim to meet the health needs of the homeless population. HCHs may also provide mobile services and aim to connect homeless individuals with supportive services such as emergency shelter, transitional housing, job training, education, and some permanent housing. Grants are also available for innovative programs that

---

[48] The outcomes discussed are not exhaustive; instead, the discussion focuses on some of the more commonly considered outcomes: improved health, reduced costs, and improved access.

[49] There are a number of outpatient facilities that provide care to underserved populations that are similar to health centers, but do not receive grants authorized in PHSA Section 330. These facilities are described in **Appendix A**.

[50] National Coalition for the Homeless at http://www.nationalhomeless.org/factsheets/health.html.

[51] P.L. 104-299 Section 330(h)(4)(A).

provide outreach and comprehensive primary health services to homeless children and children at risk of homelessness.

Health Centers for Residents of Public Housing

Health centers for residents of public housing[52] are located in public housing and aim to provide primary care to individuals who reside in public housing. These centers provide the services required of CHCs and are not required to provide specific supplemental services. These centers were authorized in 1990 because of congressional concern that public housing residents had worse health than similar (by demographic and economic status) individuals who did not reside in public housing.[53]

Migrant Health Centers

Migrant health centers provide care to migratory farm workers (persons whose principal employment is in agriculture on a seasonal basis and who establish temporary residences for work purposes) and seasonal farm workers (persons whose principal employment is in agriculture on a seasonal basis and who are not migratory agricultural workers).[54] HRSA estimates that they provide care to more than one-quarter of all migrant and seasonal farmworkers.[55] In addition to the general health center requirements, migrant health centers are required to provide certain services specific to their service population's health needs such as supportive services, environmental health services, accident prevention, and prevention and treatment of health conditions related to pesticide exposure.[56] Migrant health centers may be exempt from providing all required services, and may only operate during certain periods of the year.

Comparison of Health Center Types

Table 5 describes the four types of health centers, their target populations, the services they are required to provide, and the populations they serve. Additional services are assessed relative to the CHC service requirements (see "Health Service Requirements").

---

[52] As defined by 42 U.S.C. §1437 et. seq.

[53] P.L. 101-527, see also National Center for Health in Public Housing, "Public Housing Primary Care Program (PHPC)," press release, July 28, 2011, http://www.nchph.org/healthcenterprofiles.html.

[54] 42 U.S.C. 254b.

[55] Health Center Quality Improvement Report.

[56] 42 CFR 56.102(g).

Table 5. Comparison of Health Center Types

(2010)

Health Center Type	Target Population	Number of Sites	Additional Requirements	Population Characteristics[a]
Community Health Centers	All individuals who live in service area	7,508	Not Applicable.[b]	17,799,585[c]
Health Centers For the Homeless	Homeless individuals	2,438	Prevention and treatment services for substance abuse.	697,769 homeless patients seen; more than 20,000 of the patients served were veterans.
Health Centers for Residents of Public Housing	Individuals who reside in or near public housing	712	Must consult with public housing residents prior to applying for a grant.	172,731 patients seen. Approximately 46% of the patient population were African American and 35% were of Hispanic origin.
Migrant Health Centers	Migrant, agricultural workers	2,438	Environmental health services including sanitation services; and services related to the prevention and treatment of pesticide exposure.	799,382 patients seen in 2010; more than 90% of patients were of Hispanic origin.

Source: HRSA's Data Warehouse at http://datawarehouse.hrsa.gov/sitesdetail.aspx and HRSA, *UDS*, National Rollup Report 2010.

a. Refers to the 2010 patient population.

b. CHC-required services are considered the baseline; therefore, additional requirements are assessed relative to the requirements for CHCs.

c.   HRSA does not report number of patients seen at CHCs; this number was estimated by subtracting the number seen at the three other types of health centers from the total number of patients seen (19,469,467).

Who Uses Health Centers?

According to HRSA, health centers served 19.5 million patients in 2010. These patients were generally socioeconomically disadvantaged and uninsured or underinsured.[57] The majority of health center patients have incomes at or below the federal poverty level.[58] Nearly a quarter of patients are treated in a language other than English and the majority of health center patients are racial or ethnic minorities. In 2010, nearly one-third of health center patients were identified as African-American and/or Hispanic/Latino. Both of these rates are more than double the proportion of these groups in the overall U.S. population. **Table 6** presents some demographic characteristics of the health center patient population in 2010 including age, race, ethnicity, and insurance status.

---

[57] 2010 UDS Report.

[58] The 2010 federal poverty level was $11,139 for an individual living alone; $14,218 for a two-person family; and $22,314 for a family of four. For more information, see CRS Report RL33069, *Poverty in the United States: 2010*, by Thomas Gabe.

Table 6. Health Centers' Patients' Profile, 2010

Demographic Characteristics of Patients	Percentage of Patients Served
Income are at or below the federal poverty level	72%
Live in a rural area	50%
African-American	26%
Enrolled in Medicaid	39%
Uninsured	38%
Hispanic/Latino	35%
Age 18 and younger	34%
Enrolled in Medicare	7%
Age 65 and older	7%

Source: Department of Health and Human Services, Health Resources Services and Administration's website: http://bphc.hrsa.gov/healthcenterdatastatistics/index.html, 2010 Data Snapshot; and HRSA website: "What is a Health Center" at http://bphc.hrsa.gov/about/.

Where Are Health Centers Located?

Figure 1 shows the locations of health centers funded with PHSA Section 330 grants. These include some school-based health center locations because some grantees use Section 330 funds to support this health center type. The map generally shows, as expected, that the majority of sites are community health centers. It also shows that a number of health centers receive grants to operate multiple health center types in the same geographic area.

Figure 1. Health Center Grantee Sites

(Data as of June 2011)

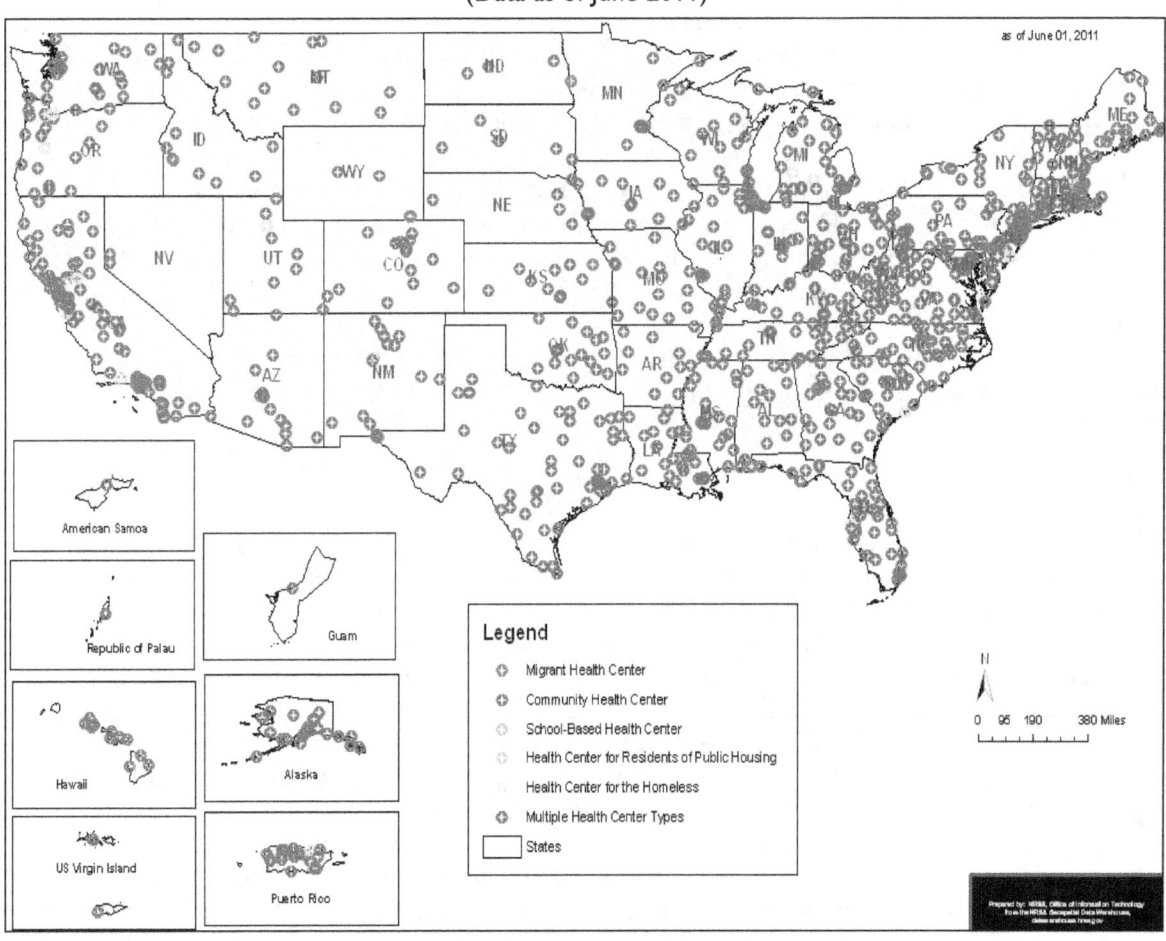

Source: HRSA Geospatial Data Warehouse.

Notes: Some entities use PHSA Section 330 funds to operate School Based Health Center even though these centers are not explicitly authorized in PHSA Section 330. The ACA created a separate grant program to support School-Based Health Centers. This program is discussed in **Appendix A**.

What Outcomes Are Associated with Health Center Use?

Researchers have found that access to health centers can improve health outcomes and reduce costs for the populations and areas they serve.[59] Research has also found that health centers may increase access to health care for generally underserved populations such as those enrolled in Medicaid and racial and ethnic minorities. This section briefly summarizes the research on the effects of health centers on health, costs, and access.

---

[59] This research is summarized in report sections "Health Outcomes" and "Cost Outcomes."

Health Outcomes

Health centers focus on preventive care and attempt to manage patients' chronic conditions. This focus may improve health by preventing disease and disease-related complications.[60] Research has found that health center patients are more likely to receive preventive health services—including pap tests and influenza vaccinations—and more likely to receive preventive screenings—including mammograms and colonoscopies—when compared to non-health center patients of similar socioeconomic status.[61] Health center patients are also more likely to have their chronic conditions—like diabetes—managed.[62] Finally, health centers aim to increase prenatal care use in low income pregnant women to reduce outcomes associated with infant mortality such as low birth weight. HRSA has found that health centers have succeeded in this effort because an increasing number of health center patients initiate prenatal care in their first trimester. This has resulted in fewer health center patients—when compared to the national average—having low birth weight babies—a major cause of infant death.[63]

Cost Outcomes

Researchers have found that health centers may lower health care costs by reducing more costly emergency department visits. GAO found that, on average, treatment at health centers is nearly one-seventh the cost of treatment of the same condition in an emergency department.[64] Given these differences in cost, health centers that are successful at reducing emergency department use may reduce health care costs. One study found that counties with health centers have lower emergency room use and that individuals who live near health centers use emergency rooms less.[65] In addition, GAO found that health centers attempt to lower emergency department use in the communities in which they operate by educating patients about services offered at health centers and by offering same day and afterhours appointments.[66]

Health centers may also reduce health care costs by preventing unnecessary hospitalizations. A number of studies have examined "ambulatory sensitive conditions," which are conditions that

[60] U.S. Government Accountability Office, *Hospital Emergency Departments: Health Center Strategies that May Help Reduce Their Use*, GAO-11-414R, April 11, 2011.

[61] Leiyu Shi et al., "Racial/Ethnic and Socioeconomic Disparities in Access to Care and Quality of Care for US Health Center Patients Compared with Non-Health Center Patients," *Journal of Ambulatory Care Management*, vol. 32, no. 4 (October-December 2009), pp. 342-350 and Leiyu Shi and Gregory D. Stevens, "The Role of Community Health Centers in Delivering Primary Care to the Underserved," *Ambulatory Care Management*, vol. 30, no. 2 (April-June 2007), pp. 159-170.

[62] Marshall H. Chin et al., "Quality of Diabetes Care in Community Health Centers," *American Journal of Public Health*, vol. 90, no. 3 (March 2000), pp. 431-434.

[63] FY2012 HRSA Budget Justification and CRS Report R41378, *The U.S. Infant Mortality Rate: International Comparisons, Underlying Factors, and Federal Programs*, by Elayne J. Heisler.

[64] See research summarized in U.S. Government Accountability Office, *Hospital Emergency Departments: Health Center Strategies that May Help Reduce Their Use*, GAO-11-414R, April 11, 2011.

[65] Md. Monir Hossain and James N. Laditka, "Using Hospitalization for Ambulatory Care Sensitive Conditions to Measure Access to Primary Health Care: An Application of Spatial Structural Equation Modeling," *International Journal of Health Geography*, vol. 8, no. 51 (August 2008) and Janice C. Probst et al., "Association Between Community Health Center and Rural Health Clinic Presence and County-Level Hospitalization Rates for Ambulatory Care Sensitive Conditions: An Analysis Across U.S. States," *BMC Health Services Research*, vol. 9, no. 134 (July 2009).

[66] U.S. Government Accountability Office, *Hospital Emergency Departments: Health Center Strategies the May Help Reduce Their Use*, GAO-11-414R, April 11, 2011.

potentially can be treated in an outpatient setting thus avoiding a hospitalization. These studies have found that in communities with health centers, individuals with these conditions were less likely to be hospitalized.[67] Health center patients enrolled in Medicaid were also less likely to be hospitalized and less likely to have an emergency room visit.[68]

Researchers have also found that patients who receive the majority of their care at health centers had lower medical costs (41% lower on average) than those who receive the majority of their care through another source.[69] Another study found the difference to be 24%,[70] while a North Carolina study found that health center users' annual health care spending was 62% less than similar patients (matched by demographic characteristics and health status) who were served in other outpatient settings.[71] Regardless of the magnitude of the difference, there appears to be consensus that health centers provide less costly health care than other outpatient settings.[72] The reasons that health centers provide less costly care are debated. The authors of the North Carolina study suggest that health centers provide health care at a lower cost because they can offer discounted services through federal programs (see "Which Federal Programs Are Available to Health Centers?"). They also suggest that health centers may provide less costly care because their providers work on a salaried basis, and so do not have financial incentives to order additional tests. In other outpatient settings this may not be the case because providers generally work under a fee-for-service model where they may receive additional remuneration for providing more services.[73] Other studies note that differences in the cost of services do not explain the difference because health centers are paid the FQHC rate, which should likely be comparable to, or higher than, the rates reimbursed in other outpatient settings. Given differing explanations on how health centers may reduce health care costs, the researchers state that health center costs may be lower because they avert more costly emergency room visits, specialty care, or hospital stays.[74]

Access to Health Care

Health centers aim to provide care to underserved populations and, in doing so, may increase health care access. By definition, health centers are located in areas with few providers including rural and inner city areas. These locations may provide to access for populations that are

---

[67] The study measured "ambulatory care sensitive conditions," which are conditions for which hospitalization could have been prevented with timely primary care. These conditions are used as a measure of access to health care and this measure has been endorsed by the Institute of Medicine, among others. See MD Monir Hossain and James N. Laditka, "Using Hospitalization for Ambulatory Care Sensitive Conditions to Measure Access to Primary Health Care: An Application of Spatial Structural Equation Modeling," *International Journal of Health Geography*, vol. 8, no. 51 (August 2008).

[68] Health Center Quality Improvement Report.

[69] Ibid.

[70] Patrick Richard et al., "Cost Savings Associated with the Use of Community Health Centers," *Journal of Ambulatory Care Management*, vol. 35, no. 1 (2012), pp. 50-59.

[71] Patrick Richard, et al., *Bending the Health Care Cost Curve in North Carolina: The Experience of Community Health Centers,* Geiger Gibson/RCHN Community Health Foundation Research Collaborative, Policy Research Brief #24, Washington, DC, August 9, 2011.

[72] See, for example, discussion in HRSA FY2012 Budget Justification and HRSA FY2013 Budget Justification.

[73] Patrick Richard, et al., *Bending the Health Care Cost Curve in North Carolina: The Experience of Community Health Centers,* Geiger Gibson/RCHN Community Health Foundation Research Collaborative, Policy Research Brief #24, Washington, DC, August 9, 2011.

[74] Patrick Richard et al., "Cost Savings Associated with the Use of Community Health Centers," *Journal of Ambulatory Care Management*, vol. 35, no. 1 (2012), pp. 50-59.

---

otherwise underserved, for example, because of geography or income. Health centers also serve a more diverse population than do office-based physicians; health center patients were more likely to be Hispanic or African American.[75] Health centers may also increase access for specific racial and ethnic groups. For example, one study found that health centers increase health care access for Asian Americans, Native Hawaiians, and other Pacific Islanders.[76] Some research has suggested that because health centers provide care to a population that might otherwise have difficultly accessing health care, health centers may reduce health disparities.[77]

Health centers are more likely to accept new patients and patients who are unable to pay for services (i.e., charity patients). Health center patients are also more likely to be enrolled in Medicaid or CHIP. As noted above health centers are required to coordinate with Medicaid and CHIP plans and are required to accept all patients regardless of their insurance status or ability to pay. Some researchers have found that private providers may not accept Medicaid patients because of the program's administrative requirements or low reimbursements rates.[78] Given this possibility, health centers may provide access to Medicaid and CHIP patients who would otherwise have difficulty finding care.

Which Federal Programs Are Available to Health Centers?

Section 330 grants, on average, cover approximately one-fifth of the cost of operating a health center;[79] the federal government provides other assistance—for example, provider recruitment and financial assistance—that may support individual health center operations. To assist with operations, health centers may employ members of the National Health Service Corps (NHSC), a program that provides scholarships and loan repayments in exchange for a period of service at a health center.[80] The federal government also provides financial support to health centers. For example, it designates health centers as Federally Qualified Health Centers (FQHCs), thereby making these facilities eligible for higher Medicare and Medicaid reimbursement rates.[81] Medicaid is the largest source of reimbursements, providing nearly 38% of all revenue for the health center program (see **Table 4**). While the amount received by an individual health center varies by the percentage of the patient population that is enrolled in Medicaid, the NACHC estimates that more than one-third of all health center revenue is from Medicaid

---

[75] Esther Hing, Roderick S. Hooker, and Jill J. Ashman, "Primary Health Care in Community Health Centers and Comparisons with Office-Based Practice," *Journal of Community Health*, vol. 36, no. 3 (2011), pp. 406-413.

[76] Rosy Chang Weir, "Use of Enabling Services by Asian American, Native Hawaiian, and Other Pacific Islander Patients at 4 Community Health Centers," *American Journal of Public Health*, vol. 100, no. 11 (November 2010), pp. 2199-2205.

[77] Health Center Quality Improvement Report.

[78] Jack Hadley and Peter Cunningham, "Availability of Safety Net Providers and Access to Care of Uninsured Persons," *Health Services Research*, vol. 39, no. 5 (October 2004), pp. 1527-1546 and Peter J. Cunningham and Ann S. O'Malley, "Do Reimbursement Delays Discourage Medicaid Participation by Physicians?" *Health Affairs*, vol. 28, no. 1 (November 18, 2008), p. w17–w28.

[79] Ibid.

[80] They may also fulfill their National Health Service Corps (NHSC) commitment at other types of facilities that provide care to the underserved.

[81] These payments are discussed in more detail in **Appendix B**; payments are considered to be "higher" than the payment rates that physician practices receive because they are cost-based and reflect a broader range of services, than do payments to physician practices. See, for example, Department of Health Policy, School of Public Health and Health Services, The George Washington University, *Quality Incentives for Federally Qualified Health Centers, Rural Health Clinics and Free Clinics: A Report to Congress*, Washington, DC, January 23, 2012.

reimbursements.[82] Health centers are also eligible for discounted prescription drugs and vaccines. Health centers may also receive additional support from grants and loans offered through other federal programs.

National Health Service Corps Providers

Health centers are automatically designated as health professional shortage areas (HPSAs) and are therefore eligible for National Health Service Corps (NHSC) providers. The NHSC provides scholarships or loan repayments to health professionals working at specific facilities in HPSAs. About half of Corps members serve in health centers,[83] making the program an important mechanism for health centers to recruit providers. In addition to the NHSC, some states may operate loan repayment programs for health professionals providing care in state designated shortage areas.[84]

J-1 Visa Waivers

Health centers may also be able to obtain providers temporarily through special waivers for J1 visa physicians. In general, foreign medical graduates who entered the country on a J-1 student visa must return to their home country for two years after they have completed their medical training (medical school and residency). J-1 visa waivers permit the two year foreign residency period to be waived if the J-1 visa holder practices primary care in a HPSA.[85] Because health centers are designated as HPSAs, a number of centers may rely on this program to recruit physicians.[86]

Federally Qualified Health Center Designation[87]

Health centers are automatically designated as Federally-Qualified Health Centers (FQHCs),[88] but must enroll as a provider in the Medicare and/or Medicaid programs to receive the higher[89]

---

[82] 2009 Health Center Chartbook.

[83] For more detailed information on the NHSC, see HRSA FY2012 Budget Justification.

[84] National Association of Community Health Centers, *The Struggle to Build a Strong Workforce at Health Centers*, Fact Sheet #0609, Washington, DC, 2009.

[85] CRS Report R40848, *Immigration Legislation and Issues in the 111th Congress*, coordinated by Andorra Bruno and http://www.raconline.org/topics/hc_providers/j1visafaq.php.

[86] This program provides a limited number of visa waivers and requires that the applicant have a three-year employment contract. For more information, see http://www.raconline.org/topics/hc_providers/j1visafaq.php.

[87] Because all health centers are eligible to be designated as Federally Qualified Health Center (FQHCs) some refer to FQHCs and health centers interchangeably.

[88] Entities that receive PHSA Section 330 funds directly or through a contract with a Section 330 grantee, may be designated as Federally Qualified Health Centers (FQHCs). When FQHCs were first established in 1989, entities that received PHSA Section 329 and Section 340 grants were also eligible to become FQHCs. The latter program is no longer authorized and the former is not currently funded.

[89] These payments are discussed in more detail in **Appendix B**; payments are considered to be "higher" than the payment rates that physician practices receive because they are cost-based and reflect a broader range of services, than do payments to physician practices. See, for example, Department of Health Policy, School of Public Health and Health Services, The George Washington University, *Quality Incentives for Federally Qualified Health Centers, Rural Health Clinics and Free Clinics: A Report to Congress*, Washington, DC, January 23, 2012.

---

reimbursement rates for services provided to patients enrolled in these programs.[90] This higher reimbursement rate is an important source of health center revenue because more than one-third of the patients seen at health centers are enrolled in Medicaid.[91] Specific FQHC Medicare and Medicaid reimbursement methodology, including recent payment changes, are described in **Appendix B**.

340B Drug Pricing Program[92]

Federal health centers are eligible to participate in the 340B Drug Pricing program, which requires drug manufacturers to provide drug discounts or rebates to 340B eligible facilities. The program is free for health centers and provides drugs at discount prices—ranging from 13% to 23% below average manufacturer price depending on the type of drug. HRSA reports that 340B eligible facilities, between FY2010 and FY2011, will receive an estimated $3 billion in drug discounts through the program.[93]

Vaccines for Children Program[94]

Health centers are eligible to participate in the Vaccines for Children Program (VFC), which provides vaccines for low income children who may not be vaccinated because of costs. The program is administered by the Centers for Disease Control and Prevention (CDC) and partially funded by Medicaid. The CDC buys the vaccines and distributes them to health departments that, in turn, distribute them to VFC providers including health centers. VFC provides free vaccines to Medicaid enrolled children and VFC eligible children (those who are uninsured, underinsured,[95] or those who are American Indian or Alaska native). Health centers are a VFC eligible provider, and provide vaccinations as part of their mission to provide primary and preventive services. The VFC program enables health centers to provide these vaccines at a lower cost to the patients and to the health center.

Federal Torts Claims Act Coverage

Health center employees and board members do not need to carry medical malpractice coverage because they are covered under the Federal Tort Claims Act (FTCA).[96] Under this program, health center employees and contractors cannot be sued for medical malpractice for care they provided that was within the scope of their health center employment. According to HRSA, in FY2010,

---

[90] Health Resources and Services Administration, *Program Assistance Letter: Process of Becoming Eligible for Medicare Reimbursements under the FQHC Benefit*, Rockville, MD, March 8, 2011.

[91] Health Center Quality Improvement Report.

[92] HRSA FY2012 Budget Justification.

[93] Ibid.

[94] This paragraph is drawn from Centers for Disease Control and Prevention, *Vaccines for Children Operations Guide*, Atlanta, GA, February 2, 2011, http://www.cdc.gov/vaccines/programs/vfc/downloads/vfc-op-guide/vfc-op-guide-all-chaptr-files.pdf.

[95] Underinsured refers to children who have private insurance coverage that does not cover vaccination or where vaccination coverage is capped at a certain amount. VFC coverage for underinsured children is only available at health centers and rural health clinics.

[96] CRS Report 95-717, *Federal Tort Claims Act (FTCA)*, by Vivian S. Chu.

103 claims were paid through the FTCA program totaling $52.6 million.[97] This program provides financial support to health centers because the center would otherwise have to pay for this coverage and would be responsible for payment and rate increases that may accompany claims made against health center providers.[98]

Ryan White HIV/AIDS Treatment Grants[99]

Health centers are eligible to receive grants authorized under parts A and C of the Ryan White AIDS program. Part A authorizes grants for primary care, access to antiretroviral therapies, and other health and supportive services. These grants are awarded to certain metropolitan areas and are used to provide care for low-income, underserved, uninsured, or underinsured individuals living with HIV/AIDS. Part C grant funds are awarded to entities to provide medical services such as testing, referrals, and clinical and diagnostic services to underserved and uninsured people living with HIV/AIDS in rural and frontier communities. In 2009, health centers received approximately $75 million in Ryan White AIDS program grants.[100]

Other Federal Grant Programs[101]

Health centers are eligible to apply for a number of federally funded grant programs including programs that seek to improve rural health and health care;[102] increase mental health and substance abuse services availability;[103] provide services to high-risk pregnant women and their infants;[104] increase health professional training at health centers;[105] and increase access to family planning services for low income families.[106] The majority of these programs are funded by discretionary appropriations and are competitive grant programs authorized in the PHSA. Programs specific to rural areas may also be administered by the U.S. Department of Agriculture (USDA) and are authorized in other acts. For example, health centers in rural areas may be eligible for USDA programs that may assist facilities with acquiring equipment or space through loan guarantees and with acquiring broadband access.[107] Health centers may also use General

---

[97] HRSA FY2013 Budget Justification.

[98] This responsibility could include both the cost of the claims and the legal costs resulting from defending providers against these claims.

[99] For more information about this program, see CRS Report RL33279, *The Ryan White HIV/AIDS Program*, by Judith A. Johnson.

[100] 2010 UDS Report.

[101] In addition to federal support and amounts collected from reimbursements, health centers may also receive support from private foundations and state or local government grants and contracts; see 2010 UDS Report.

[102] HRSA FY2013 Budget Justification; for programs through the U.S. Department of Agriculture, see http://www.rurdev.usda.gov/RD_Grants.html.

[103] CRS Report R41477, *Substance Abuse and Mental Health Services Administration (SAMHSA): Agency Overview and Reauthorization Issues*, by C. Stephen Redhead.

[104] Health Resources and Services Administration, Maternal and Child Health Bureau, "Healthy Start," accessed October 14, 2011, http://mchb.hrsa.gov/programs/healthystart/index.html.

[105] CRS Report R41390, *Discretionary Funding in the Patient Protection and Affordable Care Act (ACA)*, coordinated by C. Stephen Redhead, and CRS Report R41301, *Appropriations and Fund Transfers in the Patient Protection and Affordable Care Act (PPACA)*, by C. Stephen Redhead.

[106] CRS Report RL33644, *Title X (Public Health Service Act) Family Planning Program*, by Angela Napili.

[107] For description of these programs, see United States Department of Agriculture Rural Development, accessed October 14, 2011, http://www.rurdev.usda.gov/HCF_CF.html.

Services Administration resources to acquire real estate and dispose of property[108] and may use the Department of Housing and Urban Development's insurance program to finance facility repair and improvement.[109]

Issues for Congress

There are a number of issues facing health centers that may be of concern to Congress. These include (1) the role of health centers in health insurance expansions under the ACA; (2) the adequacy of the health center workforce; and (3) financial challenges that health centers may face. These challenges may also be interrelated; for example, health centers may be affected by the mandatory budget reductions that may be required as part of the Budget Control Act (P.L. 112-25),[110] and such budget reductions may impact the ability of health centers to provide access to care for the newly insured when the ACA is fully implemented. This section briefly summarizes these issues and discusses how some ACA changes may alleviate or exacerbate health center concerns.

Health care access has traditionally been an issue of congressional concern. For example, GAO, at congressional request, has examined Medicare and Medicaid beneficiary access to health care providers.[111] In addition, one of the purposes of ACA Title V was to improve access to and the delivery of health care services for all individuals, particularly low income, underserved, uninsured, minority, health disparity, and rural populations.[112] The health workforce and its role in providing access to traditionally underserved populations has also been an area of congressional interest. For example, one of the four mechanisms that Title V of the ACA included to improve health care access was to "increase the supply of a qualified health care workforce." The title also reauthorized a number of programs in Titles VII and VIII of the PHSA both of which focus on the workforce.

Congress, through the appropriations process for the health center program and for programs that support health centers, has an interest in the financial circumstances that health centers face. Congress may also be interested in how deficit reduction efforts and other policy changes (for example, changes in Medicare and Medicaid payments or eligibility) may affect the health center program and the financial circumstances of individual health centers. Finally, Congress may consider program changes—such as making changes to granting preference or program requirements—as a way of addressing some of the challenges that health centers face.

---

[108] See General Services Administration, Federal Real Property Utilization and Disposal at https:/// propertydisposal.gsa.gov and Personal Property for Reuse and Sale at http://www.gsa.gov/portal/category/21045.

[109] See U.S. Department of Housing and Urban Development, Property Improvement Loan Insurance (Title I) at http://www.hud.gov/offices/hsg/sfh/title/title-i.cfm.

[110] These budget reductions will be required if spending exceeds certain levels. For more information, see CRS Report R41965, *The Budget Control Act of 2011*, by Bill Heniff Jr., Elizabeth Rybicki, and Shannon M. Mahan.

[111] For discussion of Medicare beneficiary access, see U.S. Government Accountability Office, Medicare Physician Services: Utilization Trends Indicate Sustained Beneficiary Access with High and Growing Levels of Service in Some Areas of the Nation, 09-0559, August 28, 2009, http://www.gao.gov/new.items/d09559.pdf; for Medicaid, see U.S. Government Accountability Office, State and Federal Actions Have Been Taken to Improve Children's Access to Dental Services, but More Can Be Done, GAO-10-112T, October 7, 2009, http://www.gao.gov/products/GAO-10-112T.

[112] P.L. 111-148. The populations included in the purpose of this title are those that are traditionally served by health centers.

Health Centers and Health Insurance Expansion in the ACA

The ACA, by expanding health insurance coverage, may increase the number of health center patients and may increase the amount of reimbursements received. The ACA aims to expand insurance coverage by expanding Medicaid eligibility and by providing subsidies for certain individuals to obtain private insurance.[113] These changes may increase the number of individuals who access health centers and may increase the amount of reimbursements that health centers receive. Although health centers are available to the uninsured and Medicaid patients prior to the full implementation of the ACA, patients are required to pay for services based on their income (see "Fee Schedule Requirements"). Individuals who obtain private health insurance or Medicaid coverage under the ACA may have lower out of pocket costs for services received at health centers. These lower costs could increase the number of health center patients.[114] There is also evidence that individuals use more health services after obtaining insurance coverage. If this occurs after the ACA is implemented, it would also increase health center use.[115] Evidence from Massachusetts, which implemented health insurance expansions similar to those included in the ACA, suggests that health center use will increase after implementation. Massachusetts health centers reported that their patient case load increased by 7% after the state's health insurance expansions were implemented.[116] The ACA health insurance and Medicaid expansion, by potentially increasing the health center patient base, may also strain health centers' capacity to provide services. These changes may affect health care access in general and health care access for Medicaid beneficiaries in particular. This section discusses the potential impacts of Medicaid and private insurance expansion on health centers.

Health Centers and Medicaid Expansion

The ACA aims to increase health insurance coverage, in part, by expanding Medicaid enrollment.[117] Medicaid beneficiaries may seek care at health centers because some private providers may not accept Medicaid because of low reimbursement rates or administrative requirements,[118] whereas health centers are required to accept Medicaid patients. Some have speculated that the ACA's investment in health centers—in particular through the CHCF—was, in part, in recognition of the potential for an expanded health center population base.[119] Should health centers provide care to an expanded Medicaid population this would likely benefit health

---

[113]CRS Report R41664, *ACA: A Brief Overview of the Law, Implementation, and Legal Challenges*, coordinated by C. Stephen Redhead.

[114] Kaiser Commission on Medicaid and the Uninsured, *Community Health Centers: Opportunities and Challenges of Health Reform*, Issue paper, Washington, DC, August 2010.

[115] U. S Department of Health and Human Services, Health Resources and Services Administration, Bureau of Health Professions, *The Physician Workforce: Projections and Research into Current Issues Affecting Supply and Demand*, December 2008, ftp://ftp.hrsa.gov/bhpr/workforce/physicianworkforce.pdf.

[116] Kaiser Commission on Medicaid and the Uninsured, How is the Primary Care Safety Net Faring in Massachusetts? Community Health Centers in the Midst of Health Reform, Issue paper, Washington, DC, March 2009.

[117117]CRS CRS Report R41664, *ACA: A Brief Overview of the Law, Implementation, and Legal Challenges*, coordinated by C. Stephen Redhead.

[118] Peter J. Cunningham, *State Variation in Primary Care Physician Supply: Implications for Health Reform Medicaid Expansions*, Center for Studying Health System Change, No 19, Washington, DC, March 2011.

[119] Kaiser Commission on Medicaid and the Uninsured, *Community Health Centers: Opportunities and Challenges of Health Reform*, Issue paper, Washington, DC, August 2010 and Patrick Richard et al., "Cost Savings Associated with the Use of Community Health Centers," *Journal of Ambulatory Care Management*, vol. 35, no. 1 (2012), pp. 50-59.

centers because more health center patients will have services reimbursed by Medicaid.[120] The expanded service population may strain health centers' capacity to provide services, as discussed below.

Health Centers and ACA Private Insurance Expansions

Health centers are also a source of care for the uninsured, some of whom may obtain private insurance coverage under the ACA. There are some who suggest that once health center patients who were previously uninsured gain insurance coverage, they may seek private providers, which would reduce the health center service population. However, evidence from Massachusetts, which has already expanded insurance coverage, does not suggest that this will occur. Researchers found that Massachusetts health centers retained their patients after Massachusetts's insurance expansion was implemented.[121] Should this occur after the ACA insurance expansions, it would likely benefit health centers because more health center patients will have services reimbursed by private insurance,[122] which should increase health center revenue. Experts project that 9.2% of health center patients will be covered by a private insurance plan offered through the new health insurance exchanges and that this percentage should grow over time.[123]

The ACA also requires that private insurance policies offered through the newly created exchanges include access to "essential community providers"—providers that serve predominately low-income and medically underserved individuals, including health centers.[124] This would mean that health centers would be included as providers in all health insurance plans offered through the exchanges. This requirement may mean that some newly insured who were not previously health center patients may consider becoming health center patients.

The impact of the ACA when fully implemented on the health center patient base and revenue is not yet known. Furthermore, as will be discussed below, health centers face other challenges that may make it difficult to provide care to an expanded population. For example, an expanded patient base could strain health centers' capacity to provide care because some health centers have provider shortages. It is also possible that an expanded patient base may exacerbate some of the financial challenges that health centers face as reimbursements may not cover the cost of providing care[125] and some patients will remain uninsured.[126]

---

[120] Ibid.

[121] Mary Takach, *Community Health Centers and Health Reform: Highlights from a National Academy for State Health Policy Forum*, National Academy for State Health Policy, Washington, DC, October 2008.

[122] Kaiser Commission on Medicaid and the Uninsured, *Community Health Centers: Opportunities and Challenges of Health Reform*, Issue paper, Washington, DC, August 2010 and National Association of Community Health Centers, *Expanding Health Centers Under Health Care Reform: Doubling Patient Capacity and Bringing Down Costs*, Washington, DC, June 2010.

[123] Ibid.

[124] 42 U.S.C. §13031.

[125] See discussion below for "Financial Considerations" and discussion above ("Medicaid Coordination and Reimbursement Requirements") for information on how reimbursed rates relate to the cost of care.

[126] Although the ACA will expand insurance coverage some will remain uninsured even if full implementation occurs. Health centers will continue to provide access to this population and may have to rely on grant funding and sliding scale fees because some of the remaining uninsured population will not eligible for Medicaid or ACA subsidies for private plans offered through the exchange.

Health Center Workforce

One of the major challenges that health centers face is employing and retaining health care providers. The National Association of Community Health Centers (NACHC)—the advocacy group for health centers—estimates that, in 2008, health centers had 1,800 too few primary care providers (physicians, nurse practitioners, and certified nurse midwives) and 1,400 too few nurses. The organization further estimated that staffing needs would increase with health center expansion resulting in a shortage of between 15,000 and 19,000 primary care providers and between 11,000 and 14,000 nurses in 2015.[127] Health centers may have challenges recruiting and retaining staff because they are located in rural and remote areas; because there are generally declining numbers of primary care providers;[128] and because private practice options are generally more lucrative for providers.[129] Health centers have traditionally relied on the National Health Service Corps (NHSC) to recruit providers; this section discusses some of the advantages and disadvantages of that strategy. The section also discusses the advantages and disadvantages of a new ACA-authorized program—teaching health centers—to increase provider training at health centers.

National Health Service Corps Providers

To lessen the health center provider shortages, the federal government makes NHSC providers available to health centers. Recent expansions of the NHSC[130] may help health centers fill vacancies; however, appropriations in FY2011 and FY2012 indicate that these expansions may not continue.[131] More than half of all NHSC providers fulfill their service commitment in health centers, making this program an important component of the health center workforce. However, the reliance on the NHSC may create instability in the health center workforce, because the NHSC offers scholarships and loan repayments in return for a service commitment for a defined period of time. Some NHSC providers will stay beyond their service commitment; however, not all will, which may mean high turnover among health center providers. This can lead to discontinuity in care, and additional costs for health centers because of the need to continuously recruit and train providers.

Teaching Health Centers

The ACA authorizes a new program to increase medical residency training at health centers, which may help health centers recruit physicians, but may also challenge the health centers that operate these programs. The ACA authorizes teaching health centers: medical residency training programs that are located at outpatient facilities including health centers. Prior research has found

---

[127] National Association of Community Health Centers, *The Struggle to Build a Strong Workforce at Health Centers*, Fact Sheet #0609, Washington, DC, 2009.

[128] CRS Report R42029, *Physician Supply and the Patient Protection and Affordable Care Act*, by Elayne J. Heisler and Amanda K. Sarata.

[129] Roger A. Rosenblatt et al., "Shortages of Medical Personnel at Community Health Centers: Implications for Planned Expansion," *Journal of the American Medical Association*, vol. 295, no. 9 (March 2006), pp. 1042-1049.

[130] U.S. Department of Health and Human Services, "HHS Announces Record Number of National Health Service Corps Members," press release, October 13, 2011, http://www.hhs.gov/news/press/2011pres/10/20111013a.html.

[131] See discussion in HRSA section and Appendix 1 of CRS Report R41737, *Public Health Service (PHS) Agencies: Overview and Funding, FY2010-FY2012*, coordinated by C. Stephen Redhead and Pamela W. Smith.

---

that medical residents who train at health centers are more likely to be employed at health centers after they complete their training.[132] Teaching health centers may help health centers recruit physicians; however, health centers may face a number of challenges when operating residency programs. Case studies of pre-ACA teaching health centers found that operating a training program requires provider time and may reduce the number of patients a health center can see, thereby reducing health center reimbursements. These case studies also found that health centers do not receive graduate medical education payments in amounts that are high enough to support the full costs of the resident training and supervision. These case studies did show some benefits from operating training programs. For example, teaching health centers were, as expected, an important recruitment tool for health centers. These programs also connected non-primary care providers (i.e., medical specialists) with health centers because some specialists may supervise health center residents in other settings. The involvement of medical specialists in the health center may expand health center services.[133]

The ACA appropriated funding for teaching health center graduate medical education payments through FY2015. This funding may assist health centers in operating residency training programs, because programs have stated that graduate medical education payments are generally not high enough to support the cost of residency training.[134] However, efforts exist to repeal these payments (see H.R. 1216), and these payments are time limited (through FY2015). In addition, although the ACA authorized funding for grants to develop teaching health centers, no funds have been appropriated. Given that funding for teaching health center graduate medical education payments is limited and uncertain, the ACA's teaching health center program may have limited effects on health center provider recruitment and retention.

Financial Considerations

Individual health centers may have a number of financial considerations including current and future program appropriations which, in turn, affects the size of the individual health center's grant and the individual center's ability to receive continued grant funding, the impact of federal deficit reduction efforts on health centers, changes in state funding available for health centers, and the potential effects of ACA care coordination efforts on health centers. Between 2000 and 2010, the health center program's appropriation increased; however, given recent focus on deficit reduction, it is unclear whether these expansions will continue. Whether the health center program should be expanded or contracted is difficult to assess. Further, assessments about the appropriate size of the health center program may also change depending on ACA implementation, economic conditions in general, and a number of other factors. Given these challenges, it is beyond the scope of this report to assess whether the size of the health center program is appropriate. Instead, this section discusses changes in federal funding for health center program and state funding for individual health centers and how the ACA may affect individual health center finances.[135] Specifically, state and local funding is a large source of support for

---

[132] Krystal Knight et al., *Health Centers' Contributions to Training Tomorrow's Physicians*, National Association of Community Health Centers, Washington, DC, August 2010.

[133] Ibid.

[134] U.S. Department of Health and Human Services, Health Resources and Services Administration, "HHS Announces New Teaching Health Centers Graduate Medical Education Program," press release, January 25, 2011, http://www.hrsa.gov/about/news/pressreleases/110125teachinghealthcenters.html.

[135] State funding for health centers varies by state and the number of health centers also vary; therefore, it is not possible to assess the amount of state funding provided to health centers relative to a health center's total budget.

---

health centers (see **Table 4**), although the amount of funding an individual health center receives varies. A number of states face fiscal challenges and have reduced their financial support of health centers, but the ACA may provide additional support to health centers in the form of increased reimbursements and reimbursements for care coordination, which many health centers currently provide, but without reimbursement.

Health Center Appropriations and the Community Health Center Fund

The ACA included the CHCF, but it is unclear whether this will increase health center appropriation levels. As shown in **Table 3**, the health center program has grown in the past decade. This growth included funding increases for individual centers and funding for more centers. ARRA continued these expansions, but appropriations for health centers may no longer be increased as occurred in FY2011 and FY2012.[136] As discussed above, the ACA appropriated CHCF may be rescinded or used in place of the amounts that had been appropriated for the health center program through the annual appropriations process. To a certain extent this occurred in FY2011 and FY2012 when, as part of budget reduction efforts, $600 million of the CHCF was used as part of the health center appropriation. Advocates note that this phenomenon resulted in fewer New Access Point grants (i.e., grants to establish new health centers) being awarded as HRSA used appropriated funds to support health centers already in existence including those created using ARRA funds.[137] This may indicate that the federal government's focus has shifted to maintaining the program—rather than continuing program expansions—as congressional concern has increasingly focused on deficit reduction.

Health Center Appropriations and the Budget Control Act

Health center appropriations may also be affected by the possibility of budget reduction provisions contained in deficit reduction proposals. The Budget Control Act (BCA, P.L. 112-25) required that a deficit reduction plan be enacted to avoid mandatory budget reductions (called sequestration). No such plan was enacted, so mandatory reductions are set to begin in 2013.[138] Although budget reductions are limited to 2% for health centers, it is not clear whether this limit will apply to CHCF funds.[139] In addition, there are no limits on the budget reductions for some of the programs that provide financial or in-kind support to health centers, such as the NHSC and

---

[136] Funding increases discussed do not take into account inflation nor do they take into account medical inflation, which is generally higher than general inflation.

[137] Sara Rosenbaum and Peter Shin, *Community Health Centers and the Economy: Assessing Center's Role in Immediate Job Creation Efforts*, Geiger Gibson/ RCHN Community Health Foundation Research Collaborative, Policy Research Brief #25, Washington, DC, September 14, 2011. In August of 2010, HRSA announced that there would be up to $250 million available to support New Access Point grants and estimated that it would support 350 new health center delivery sites in FY2011. However, in August of 2011, HRSA announced that it had awarded $28.8 million for New Access Point grants. See U.S. Department of Health and Human Services, "HHS Announces Availability of Health Center New Access Point Grants," press release, August 9, 2010, http://www.hhs.gov/news/press/2010pres/08/20100809a.html, and U.S. Department of Health and Human Services, "HHS Awards Affordable Care Act Funds to Expand Access to Health Care," press release, August 9, 2011, http://www.hhs.gov/news/press/2011pres/08/20110809a.html.

[138] CRS Report R41965, *The Budget Control Act of 2011*, by Bill Heniff Jr., Elizabeth Rybicki, and Shannon M. Mahan.

[139] This determination will be made by the Office of Management and Budget. CRS Report R42050, *Budget "Sequestration" and Selected Program Exemptions and Special Rules*, coordinated by Karen Spar. This determination will be made by the Office of Management and Budget.

---

the Ryan White HIV/AIDS Program. Should sequestration occur as scheduled, health centers could be affected both by reductions to their program budgets and by reductions to programs that provide additional revenue, staffing, or services to health centers.

Health Center Funding and ACA Care Coordination Initiatives

The ACA may provide additional reimbursements to support care coordination. Health centers may coordinate care in ways that reduce health care costs to the system overall, but may have little or no monetary benefit to the health center doing the care coordination. For example, GAO found that health centers employ a number of strategies to reduce emergency department use, which, as noted above, is more expensive than care provided in a health center.[140] Reduced emergency department use may yield savings to third party payers or hospitals, but would not yield savings to health centers. The opposite may actually be true, whereby health centers employ strategies such as care coordination and case management, which may not be reimbursed by third party payers. Some health centers are concerned about sustaining these efforts,[141] and funding constraints may make it more difficult for health centers to provide these services. However, the ACA may make it more feasible for health centers to sustain these efforts because the law includes programs that may provide additional reimbursements for care coordination activities.[142] Specifically, health centers are eligible for increased reimbursements under Medicare to increase primary care and care coordination[143] and may participate in accountable care organizations that aim to increase care coordination across health providers.[144]

Health Center Funding and State Funding Availability[145]

As discussed above, future federal funding for health centers is in flux; in addition, a number of states are reducing their funding for health centers because of state-level fiscal constraints. As shown in **Table 4**, state funding is an important source of revenue for health centers; however, state funding available for health center varies by state and is declining. Specifically, in November of 2010, the NACHC, in a letter to the Secretary of HHS, noted that state funding for health centers had declined 42% since 2008. The organization also noted that some state policymakers have argued that less state funding is needed for health centers because of the

---

[140] U.S. Government Accountability Office, *Hospital Emergency Departments: Health Center Strategies that May Help Reduce Their Use*, GAO-11-414R, April 11, 2011.

[141] Ibid.

[142] See discussion of these efforts in CRS Report R41474, *Accountable Care Organizations and the Medicare Shared Savings Program*, by Amanda K. Sarata, and section on "PPACA Provisions Targeting Physician Productivity" in CRS Report R42029, *Physician Supply and the Patient Protection and Affordable Care Act*, by Elayne J. Heisler and Amanda K. Sarata.

[143] Rebecca Adams, "HHS Announces Community Health Center Grant Opportunity," *CQ HEALTHBEAT NEWS*, June 6, 2011 and U.S. Department of Health and Human Services, "Affordable Care Act to Support Quality Improvement and Access to Primary Care for More Americans," press release, September 20, 2011, http://www.hhs.gov/news/press/2011pres/09/20110929b.html.

[144] CRS Report R41474, *Accountable Care Organizations and the Medicare Shared Savings Program*, by Amanda K. Sarata.

[145] Unless otherwise noted, this paragraph is drawn from National Association of Community Health Centers, *Calculating the Cost: State Budgets and Community Health Centers*, State Policy Report #39, Washington, DC, November 2011 and Letter from Tom Van Coverden, President and CEO, National Association of Community Health Centers, to Honorable Kathleen Sebelius, Secretary, U.S. Department of Health and Human Services, December 3, 2010, http://www.nachc.com/client/Leter%20to%20Secretary%20Sebelius%20-%20120310.pdf.

---

federal government's investment in the program through ARRA and ACA appropriations. In contrast, advocates argue that such state funding is still needed and that these state funding reductions coupled with the uncertainty of the CHCF may mean reductions in the services that health centers can provide. Advocates also argue that much of the reduced health care costs attributed to health center usage accrues to Medicaid—a joint federal-state program—so states realize some cost savings from health centers, which should justify state investment in health centers. A November 2011 report indicates that states continue to reduce their funding for health centers. The report surveyed state funding levels for state FY2012 and found a 15% decline from state FY2011. In addition, some states that have historically supported health centers have, because of state budget concerns, withdrawn this support.[146] Advocates argue that these recent declines in state funding for health centers may continue and, when coupled with decreasing federal appropriations for health centers, may strain health center finances.

Concluding Observations

Health centers serve a predominantly low-income medically underserved population who have limited or no access to health care. Research has shown that health centers improve health care access and improve health for the underserved populations they target. In doing so, health centers may reduce the use of more costly emergency department services thereby reducing health care costs. The federal government supports health centers through the health center program that awards grants to plan, operate, and expand health centers and through programs that provide recruitment and financial incentives including increased reimbursements through the FQHC designation. Health center appropriations have increased over the past decade, but it is unclear whether these increases will continue. There are a number of issues facing both the health center program and individual health centers that may be of concern to Congress. On the program side, Congress may be concerned about the program's appropriation level and the impact of federal deficit reduction efforts on the health center program. For individual health centers, Congress may be concerned about provider vacancies and the role that individual health centers may play in providing health access when the ACA is fully implemented.

---

[146] Six states their funding; 19 states reduced their funding; and 15 states did not provide funding. National Association of Community Health Centers, *Calculating the Cost: State Budgets and Community Health Centers*, State Policy Report #39, Washington, DC, November 2011.and Dawn McKinney et al., *Entering the Era of Reform: The Future of State Funding for Health Centers*, National Association of Community Health Centers, State Policy Report #33, Washington, DC, October 2010, http://www.nachc.com/client/State%20Funding%20Report-%20Final.pdf.

Appendix A. Other Federal Programs that May Provide Primary Care to the Underserved

The federal government supports facilities that provide primary care to low-income or otherwise medically underserved populations through a number of facilities that are similar to health centers, but are not authorized in PHSA Section 330. For example, the ACA authorized funding for school-based health centers and nurse-managed health clinics. Both of these facilities serve underserved populations, but have different requirements than facilities authorized in PHSA Section 330. The federal government also provides support for facilities that provide care to targeted populations such as American Indians and Alaska Natives and Native Hawaiians, facilities located in rural areas, facilities that provide mental health services, and facilities that provide free care. This appendix describes these types of facilities, their authorization, and program requirements.

School-Based Health Centers

School-based health centers (SBHCs) are facilities located on or near school grounds that provide age-appropriate comprehensive primary health care services to students regardless of their ability to pay.[147] SBHCs may be located at public, private, charter, or parochial schools and must open, at a minimum, during school hours.[148] Prior to ACA, HRSA funded SBHCs through its Section 330 appropriation.[149] ACA authorized separate SBHC grants in Section 339Z-1 of the PHSA and appropriated $200 million ($50 million annually) from FY2010 to FY2013 to support grants for SBHC construction and renovation.[150] Although ACA authorized grants for SBHC operation, funding was not appropriated in FY2011 or FY2012, and is not proposed for FY2013.[151] Despite the lack of an explicit SBHC operating grant program, some Section 330 grantees may operate SBHCs. HRSA estimates that there are 358 SBHCs.[152]

---

[147] U.S. Government Accountability Office, *School-Based Health Centers: Available Information on Federal Funding*, 11-18R, October 8, 2010, http://www.gao.gov/new.items/d1118r.pdf.

[148] Section 2110(c)(9) of the Social Security Act defines a sponsoring facility as: a) a hospital; b) a public health department; c) a community health center; d) a non-profit health care agency; e) a local educational agency; or f) a program administered by the Indian Health Service or the Bureau of Indian Affairs or operated by an Indian tribe or a tribal organization.

[149] HRSA recognizes children as an underserved population and permitted SBHCs to apply for health center funding. See Budget Period Renewal Non-Competing Continuation Funding Under the Consolidated Health Centers Program Announcement Number: 5-H80-06-001, Catalog of Federal Domestic Assistance (CFA) No. 93.224, Program Guidance, Fiscal Year 2006. U.S. Department of Health and Human Services, Health Resources and Services Administration, Bureau of Primary Health Care, July 7, 2005, p. 3 (footnote 1) and page 4, at ftp://ftp.hrsa.gov/bphc/docs/2005pins/2005-20.pdf

[150] HRSA Press Office: HHS Announces Availability of $100 million for School-based Health Centers, October 4, 2010 at http://www.hrsa.gov/about/news/pressreleases/101004schoolbasedhealthcenters.html; and the awarding of this funding, at http://www.hhs.gov/news/press/2011pres/12/20111208a.html. H.R. 1214 would repeal this funding and rescind any unobligated funding.

[151] HRSA FY2013 Budget Justification.

[152] HRSA Data Warehouse.

Nurse-Managed Health Clinics

Nurse-Managed Health Centers (NMHCs) are centers that provide comprehensive primary care and wellness services to underserved populations where nurses provide the majority of health services. NMHCs are required to serve the entire population in the area in which they are located and must have an advisory committee similar to those required for Section 330 health centers. NHMCs provide wellness services, prenatal care, disease prevention, management of chronic conditions like asthma, hypertension and diabetes, and health education. Some also provide dental and mental health services.[153] ACA authorized grants to support NMHCs in PHSA Section 330A-1. In FY2010, HHS awarded $15 million to provide 3 years of support for 10 NHMCs.[154] Grantees are required to submit a sustainability plan for operation after the federal grant period is complete in 2013.[155]

Community Mental Health Centers

Community mental health centers (CMHC)[156] are licensed facilities that provide mental health services. These facilities are required to provide mental health services that are tailored to the needs of children and adults (including the elderly) who have a serious mental illness. These facilities are also required to provide services to individuals that have been discharged from inpatient treatment at a mental health facility. Among the required services, CMHCs must provide emergency services; day treatment or other partial hospitalization services; psychosocial rehabilitation services; and screening for admission into state mental health facilities. The ACA required that CMHCs provide less than 40% of its services to Medicare beneficiaries.[157]

CHMCs received approximately $400 million in funding in FY2009 through FY2011 through Substance Abuse and Mental Health Services Administration (SAMHSA) block grants. In addition, CMHCs are eligible for SAMHSA substance abuse prevention and treatment grants, and HHS grants awarded through the Social Service Block Grant.[158] CMHCs also receive reimbursements from Medicare and Medicaid for covered services provided to beneficiaries enrolled in these programs. According to CMS there are 639 Medicare approved CMHCs.[159]

---

[153] Tina Hansen-Turton, *NNCC 2010 Annual Report*, National Nursing Centers Consortium, Philadelphia, PA, http://www.nncc.us/site/pdf/publications/2010AnnualReport.pdf.

[154] Department of Health and Human Services, "Sebelius Announces New $250 Million Investment to Strengthen Primary Health Care Workforce," press release, June 16, 2010, http://www.hhs.gov/news/press/2010pres/06/20100616a.html.

[155] Ibid.

[156] As defined in 42 U.S.C. §1395x.

[157] P.L. 111-152 added this requirement effective April 1, 2011. CMS is also proposing to establish conditions of participation—requirements for Medicare providers—for new CMHCs. See Medicare Press Release. "Medicare proposes new standards for Community Mental Health Centers." June 16, 2011, http://www.cms.gov/apps/media/press/release.asp?Counter=3982&intNumPerPage=10&checkDate=&checkKey=&srchType=1&numDays=3500&srchOpt=0&srchData=&keywordType=All&chkNewsType=1%2C+2%2C+3%2C+4%2C+5&intPage=&showAll=&pYear=&year=&desc=false&cboOrder=date.

[158] CRS Report 94-953, *Social Services Block Grant: Background and Funding*, by Karen E. Lynch.

[159] Office of Legislation, Centers for Medicare & Medicaid Services, April 1, 2011.

Native Hawaiian Health Care

The federal government supports the Native Hawaiian Health Care System (NHHCS), which is composed of five grantees and the Papa Ola Lokahi, a consortium of health care organizations that provide primary care, health promotion, and disease prevention services to Native Hawaiians. This population often faces cultural, financial, and geographic barriers to accessing health care services. The NHHCS was originally authorized under the Native Hawaiian Health Care Act of 1988 (P.L. 100-579), which was reauthorized through FY2010 in the ACA.[160] The NHHCS is not a grant program under Section 330 of the Public Health Service Act, but the system receives funding through the health center appropriation.[161] In FY2010, NHHCS provided medical and enabling services, such as transportation and translation services, to more than 8,400 people.[162]

Tribal Health Centers

Indian Tribes (ITs), Tribal Organization (TOs), and Urban Indian Organizations (UIOs)[163] may receive funds from the Indian Health Service (IHS) to operate health centers for American Indians or Alaska Natives. Although tribal health centers may be similar to health centers funded under Section 330 grants they are not subject to Section 330 requirements. For example, they are not required to provide services to all individuals in their service area. They are also not required to seek payments or reimbursements on behalf of the clients they see because IHS provides services to all eligible American Indians and Alaska Natives free of charge. Tribal health centers—those operated by an IT, a TO, or a UIO—may be designated as Federally Qualified Health Centers (FQHCs)[164] and receive the Medicare and Medicaid FQHC payment rate (See **Appendix B**).

ITs, TOs, and UIOs may also apply for and receive funds under Section 330 of the PHSA; however, should an entity receive Section 330 funds it would be subject to all Section 330 requirements (i.e., would be require to provide services to non-American Indians and Alaska Natives). Tribal health centers that receive Section 330 grants are also required to ensure that funds received from IHS are only used to provide services to IHS-eligible individuals.

Rural Health Clinics

Rural health clinics (RHCs) are outpatient primary care facilities located in rural and medically underserved areas. These facilities receive higher Medicare and Medicaid payments—similar to the FQHC payment rate—for services provided to beneficiaries enrolled in the Medicare and

---

[160] This program was reauthorized, through FY2019, in PPACA, see CRS Report R41630, *The Indian Health Care Improvement Act Reauthorization and Extension as Enacted by the ACA: Detailed Summary and Timeline*, by Elayne J. Heisler.

[161] The NHHCS program has funded from the Consolidated Health Centers budget line annually since 1997. Personal correspondence with HRSA's Office of Legislation on January 20, 2011.

[162] Health Resources and Services Administration, *The Health Center Program: Special Populations* at http://bphc.hrsa.gov/about/specialpopulations.htm and HRSA FY2013 Budget Justification.

[163] Indian Tribes and Tribal Organizations must be operating facilities under the authority of the Indian Self-Determination and Education Assistance Act (P.L. 93-638); and Urban Indian Organizations must receive grants authorized under Title V of the Indian Health Care Improvement Act. For more information, see CRS Report R41630, *The Indian Health Care Improvement Act Reauthorization and Extension as Enacted by the ACA: Detailed Summary and Timeline*, by Elayne J. Heisler.

[164] These facilities received the ability to be designated as FQHCs in P.L. 103-66.

Medicaid programs. RHCs are similar to health centers except that they (1) do not receive federal grants; (2) may be operated by for-profit entities, (3) are not required to provide services to individuals regardless of ability to pay; and (4) are not required to offer a sliding scale fee schedule.[165]

Free Clinics

Free clinics are outpatient facilities that provide medical, dental, and behavioral health services to underserved populations that are primarily uninsured. Free clinics are tax-exempt organizations that provide health care to individuals regardless of their ability to pay and are not permitted to charge for services.[166] In general, free clinic funding comes from donations (both monetary and in-kind), religious groups, foundations and corporations.[167] There are more than 1,200 free clinics[168] that provide services to a population that is similar to that served by health centers.[169] Free clinics do not receive funding from HRSA, but may participate in the Free Clinics Medical Malpractice Program administered by HRSA that provides liability coverage to health care providers at free clinics.[170]

FQHC Look-Alikes

FQHC look-alikes are facilities that meet the criteria to receive a health center grant, but do not receive a grant because Section 330 funding is not available. The FQHC look-alike program began in 1991 to support the demand for new health centers.[171] HRSA and CMS can designate certain facilities as "FQHC look-alikes," making these facilities eligible for certain federal programs (e.g., the NHSC and the 340B drug discount program)[172] available to health centers and for the FQHC payment rate. To be designated as an FQHC look-alike, a facility submits an application to HRSA, the agency reviews the application and then recommends to CMS which facilities should be designated as FQHC look-alikes. As of January 2012, HRSA reported that there were 107 FQHC look-alikes.[173]

---

[165] Health Resources and Services Administration, Department of Health and Human Services, *Comparison of the Rural Health Clinic and Federally Qualified Health Center Programs*, Revised, Rockville, MD, June 2006, http://www.ask.hrsa.gov/downloads/fqhc-rhccomparison.pdf.

[166] 42 U.S.C. §233.

[167] Ibid.

[168] See http://www.freeclinics.us/.

[169] Darnell, Julie S. "Free Clinics in the United States: A Nationwide Survey." *Archives of Internal Medicine*, vol. 170 (June 2010), pp. 946-953.

[170] See http://bphc.hrsa.gov/ftca/freeclinics/; this coverage is similar to the Federal Torts Claims Act coverage discussed above, see "Federal Torts Claims Act Coverage."

[171] Section 1905 of the Social Security Act for Medicaid; and Section 1861(aa)(4) of the Social Security Act for Medicare.

[172] See descriptions of these programs in the report sections "National Health Service Corps Providers" and "340B Drug Pricing Program".

[173] Email from HHS, Office of Legislation, January 26, 2012.

Appendix B. Medicare and Medicaid Payments and Beneficiary Cost Sharing for Health Center Services

All health centers can be designated as federally qualified health centers (FQHCs)[174] upon enrolling as a provider in the Medicare and Medicaid programs.[175] The FQHC designation makes

Section 330 grantees (among others, see text box) eligible for Medicare and Medicaid reimbursements rates that are generally higher than the reimbursement rates for comparable services provided in a physician's office.[176] The FQHC designation was created to ensure that Medicare and Medicaid reimbursements cover the costs of providing services so that Section 330

Social Security Act FQHC Definition

FQHC means (1) an entity that is receiving a PHSA Section 330 grant or is receiving funding through a contract with a PHSA Section 330 grant recipient; (2) an entity that meets the requirements to receive a PHSA Section 330 grant as determined by HRSA; (3) an entity that was treated by the Secretary of HHS as a comprehensive federally funded health center for the purposes of Medicare Part B as of January 1, 1990; or (4) an outpatient program or facility operated by an Indian Tribe, Tribal Organization, or Urban Indian Organization receiving funds authorized in the Indian Health Care Improvement Act.

Source: §1861 I(aa)(4 of the Social Security Act, 42 U.S.C. §1395x and §1905(l)(2)(B), 42 U.S.C. §1396d.

---

grant funds are not used to subsidize these costs.[177] This appendix describes Medicare and Medicaid payments to FQHCs and ACA-required changes to Medicare FQHC payments.

---

[174] The Medicaid payment designation began in 1990 in the Omnibus Budget Reconciliation Act (OBRA) of 1989 (P.L. 101-239). The FQHC payment rate for Medicare was implemented in 1992 in Department of Health and Human Services, "Medicare Program: Payment for Federally Qualified Health Center Services," 57 *Federal Register* 24,961, June 12, 1992 and 61 *Federal Register* 14,640, April 3, 1996.

[175] A Section 330 grantee can operate facilities at multiple sites, each of these sites must enroll as an FQHC. See Health Resources and Services Administration, *Program Assistance Letter: Process of Becoming Eligible for Medicare Reimbursements under the FQHC Benefit*, Rockville, MD, March 8, 2011.

[176] These payments are considered to be "higher" than the payment rates that physician practices receive because they are cost-based and reflect a broader range of services, than do payments to physician practices. See, for example, Department of Health Policy, School of Public Health and Health Services, The George Washington University, *Quality Incentives for Federally Qualified Health Centers, Rural Health Clinics and Free Clinics: A Report to Congress*, Washington, DC, January 23, 2012.

[177] See discussion in National Association of Community Health Centers, *Emerging Issues in the FQHC Prospective Payment System*, Washington, DC, September 2011 and U.S. Government Accountability Office, *Medicare Payments to Federally Qualified Health Centers*, GAO-10-576R, July 30, 2010.

Medicare Payments to Health Centers

Health centers are paid an all-inclusive payment rate for most services provided to Medicare beneficiaries. It is intended to reflect the cost of all services provided to a beneficiary during a "covered visit" regardless of the specific services provided (see text box).[178] The all-inclusive payment rate is calculated by dividing the total estimated allowable costs (with certain limits that take into account the reasonable costs

> ### What Is a Covered Visit?
>
> Medicare pays FQHCs an all-inclusive rate for most services received during a "covered visit."
>
> Medicare defines a "visit" as a face-to-face encounter between a patient and a provider (physician, physician assistant, nurse practitioner, nurse midwives, visiting nurse, clinical psychologist, or clinic social worker) where an FQHC service is provided (e.g., a medical, mental health service, diabetes self-management training, or medical nutrition therapy). A "visit" may include services received from more than one health professional in a single day at the same location; however, a patient may have more than one visit type. For example, a patient can have a medical visit and a mental health visit in the same day or may have a medical visit and a diabetes self management training visit in the same day. The facility may receive a separate all-inclusive payment rate for each of these visit types.
>
> **Source**: U.S. Department of Health and Human Services, Center for Medicare and Medicaid Services, *Medicare Claims Process Manual*, Chapter 9- Rural Health Clinics/Federally Qualified Health Centers, Baltimore, MD, November 12, 2010, p. 16, https://www.cms.gov/manuals/downloads/clm104c09.pdf.

for providing a service, productivity, and payment limits) by the number of total number of visits for services (see text box for definition of visits). The rate includes services provided by physicians and other providers and the supplies used to provide these services.[179] The all-inclusive rate does not apply for certain preventive services including pneumococcal and influenza vaccines and their administration; instead these services are billed separately and reimbursed at 100% of the reasonable cost of providing the service. The all-inclusive payment rate also does not include certain diagnostic tests such as x-rays and laboratory tests, which are billed separately.[180] FQHCs are reimbursed based on estimated costs, this payment is then adjusted at the end of the year to account for the actual costs of providing services. These reconciled amounts are subject to payment limits, which are updated each year by a measure of price inflation. The all inclusive payment rate is also updated annually and is adjusted to take into account urban and rural differences in the costs of providing care.[181]

Medicare beneficiaries are subject to different deductible and cost sharing requirements for services provided at FQHCs. Specifically, the Medicare Part B deductible does not apply for

[178] Health Resources and Services Administration, *Program Assistant Letter: Process for Becoming Eligible for Medicare Reimbursements Under the FQHC Program Benefit*, 2011-4, Rockville, MD, March 8, 2011.

[179] U.S. Government Accountability Office, *Medicare Payments to Federally Qualified Health Centers*, GAO-10-576R, July 30, 2010.

[180] Ibid.

[181] For example, the 2012 urban per visit payment for an FQHC is $126.98 while the rural per visit payment limit is $109.90. See CMS Transmittal 2343, SUBJECT: Announcement of Medicare Rural Health Clinics (RHCs) and Federally Qualified Health Centers (FQHCs) Payment Rate Increases, November 4, 2011, http://www.cms.gov/transmittals/downloads/R2343CP.pdf. CMS Manual System. Note: If the FQHC is located within a Metropolitan Statistical Area (MSA) or New England County Metropolitan area (NECMA), then the urban limit applies. If the FQHC is not in an MSA or NECMA and cannot be classified as a large or other urban area, the rural limit applies. Rural FQHCs cannot be reclassified into an urban area (as determined by the Bureau of Census) for FQHC payment limit purposes.

FQHC services.[182] Beneficiaries—with some exceptions[183]—must pay the 20% copayment for Medicare services.

ACA Payment Changes

Recent studies have indicated that Medicare reimbursements may not be sufficient to cover the costs of providing services;[184] therefore, the ACA requires changes to how FQHCs are paid for services provided to Medicare beneficiaries. Specifically, the ACA required that Medicare develop a prospective payment system (PPS) for FQHCs that, when implemented in 2014, would eliminate the all-inclusive payment rate and may better align Medicare payments with the cost of providing services. In order to develop this system, the ACA required that, as of January 1, 2011, FQHCs report every service provided during a Medicare-covered patient visit using the appropriate Healthcare Common Procedure Coding System (HCPCS) code.[185] The HCPCS codes will then be used to develop a PPS that reflects the cost of providing services to Medicare beneficiaries.

The ACA also required that Medicare preventive services and the initial exam for new Medicare beneficiaries be provided without copayments.[186] This differs from the general Medicare beneficiary copayment of 20% of the fee charged by the health center.

Mental Health Service Payment Changes

The Medicare Improvements for Patients and Providers Act of 2008 (MIPPA, P.L. 110-275) also changed Medicare reimbursement for mental health services at FQHCs. Previously, Medicare reimbursements were limited at 62.5% of the reasonable costs for outpatient mental health services; however, this limit will be phased out by January 1, 2014.[187]

---

[182] For discussion of FQHC services, see discussion in report section "Health Service Requirements".

[183] FQHCs can waive collection of all or part of the coinsurance, depending upon the beneficiary's ability to pay.

[184] See discussion in report section "Medicaid Coordination and Reimbursement Requirements" and U.S. Government Accountability Office, *Medicare Payments to Federally Qualified Health Centers*, GAO-10-576R, July 30, 2010.

[185] Healthcare Common Procedure Coding System (HCPCS) is used to standardize the identification of medical services, supplies and equipment. It is used when billing the Medicare and Medicaid programs. Source: https://www.cms.gov/MedHCPCSGenInfo/20_HCPCS_Coding_Questions.asp

[186] CRS Report R40978, *Medicare Coverage of Clinical Preventive Services*, by Sarah A. Lister and Kirsten J. Colello, and CRS Report R41196, *Medicare Provisions in the Patient Protection and Affordable Care Act (PPACA): Summary and Timeline*, coordinated by Patricia A. Davis.

[187] U.S. Department of Health and Human Services, Center for Medicare and Medicaid Services, *Medicare Claims Process Manual*, Chapter 9- Rural Health Clinics/Federally Qualified Health Centers, Baltimore, MD, November 12, 2010, p. 18, https://www.cms.gov/manuals/downloads/clm104c09.pdf and CRS Report RL34592, *P.L. 110-275: The Medicare Improvements for Patients and Providers Act of 2008*, coordinated by Hinda Chaikind.

Medicaid Payments

Medicaid uses a PPS to reimburse FQHCs for services provided to Medicaid beneficiaries.[188] The PPS establishes a predetermined per-visit payment rate for each FQHC based on costs of services. The PPS was established based on cost report data in FY1999 and FY2000 and is updated annually for medical inflation.[189] The state, in turn, receives the appropriate federal matching amount. States are also required to adjust PPS payment rates based on any changes in the scope of services provided at the FQHC. States are not required to use the PPS to reimburse FQHCs, but they may not reimburse an FQHC less than it would have received under the PPS.[190] In 2010, approximately 20 states did not use the PPS and instead used an alternative payment methodology (APM) to reimburse FQHCs under Medicaid.[191] States are also required to supplement FQHCs that subcontract (directly or indirectly) with Medicaid Managed Care Entities (MCEs). These supplemental payments are supposed to make up the difference, if any, between the payment received by the FQHC from the MCE and the Medicaid payment that the FQHC would be entitled to under the PPS or the APM.[192] The ACA did not include changes in Medicaid FQHC reimbursement policy.

Author Contact Information

Elayne J. Heisler
Analyst in Health Services
eheisler@crs.loc.gov, 7-4453

Acknowledgments

This report benefited from comments received from Barbara English, Paulette C. Morgan, and Amanda K. Sarata.

---

[188] This was established under the Medicare, Medicaid, and SCHIP Benefits Improvement and Protection Act of 2000 (BIPA), P.L. 106-554); see CRS Report RL30718, *Medicaid, SCHIP, and Other Health Provisions in H.R. 5661: Medicare, Medicaid, and SCHIP Benefits Improvement and Protection Act of 2000*, by Jean Hearne and Evelyne P. Baumrucker. Prior to the PPS, Medicaid used an all-inclusive rate.

[189] U.S. Government Accountability Office, *Medicare Payments to Federally Qualified Health Centers*, GAO-10-576R, July 30, 2010.

[190] Ibid.

[191] National Association of Community Health Centers, *Emerging Issues in the FQHC Prospective Payment System*, Washington, DC, September 2011.

[192] Letter providing initial guidance on the new Medicaid prospective payment system, Jan. 19, 2001 at http://www.cms.hhs.gov/smdl/downloads/smd011901d.pdf

www.ingramcontent.com/pod-product-compliance
Lightning Source LLC
Chambersburg PA
CBHW080625290526
45790CB00007B/2934